REVIEW OF QUALIFICATIONS FOR

16–19 YEAR OLDS

WITHDRAWN

Contents

SECTION 1

Background and introduction

Terms of reference and purposes of the Review

1.1 On 10 April 1995 I was invited 'to consider and advise the Secretaries of State for Education and Employment and for Wales on ways to strengthen, consolidate and improve the framework of 16–19 qualifications'.

1.2 I was asked 'to have particular regard to the need to:

■ Maintain the rigour of General Certificate of Education (GCE) Advanced (A) levels.

■ Continue to build on the current development of General National Vocational Qualifications (GNVQs) and National Vocational Qualifications (NVQs).

■ Increase participation and achievement in education and training and minimise wastage.

■ Prepare young people for work and higher education; and

■ Secure maximum value for money.'

1.3 In addition to the remit, the Secretary of State for Education asked a number of questions.

■ 'Is there scope for measures to achieve greater coherence and breadth of study post-16 without compromising standards; and how can we strengthen our qualifications framework further?

■ Why is it that many students do not complete their courses? Can school and college resources be better used to enable young people to take full advantage of the ability to mix and match qualifications to suit their needs and abilities?

■ Should we make sure that our most able pupils are stretched and suitably rewarded for excellence? And should we encourage core skills, which are already an essential part of GNVQs, as part of the programme of study for more 16–19 year olds?'

1.4 Although my remit was jointly from the Secretaries of State for Education, Employment and Wales, during the review I have also consulted with and taken into account the interests of Northern Ireland, where the same qualifications are offered. The remit did not cover Scotland, where the education system is different, but some of the recommendations I make in this Report cover UK-wide initiatives, such as the National Record of Achievement, Modern Apprenticeships and Youth Training.

1.5   As I saw them, the purposes of the Review were to:

■ Provide diversity of opportunity and informed choice for learners.

■ Motivate, and recognise achievement by, people of all ability levels.

■ Ensure standards are rigorous, challenge expectations, and encourage excellence.

■ Increase the coherence of the national qualifications framework, reduce its complexity, and make it more easily understandable by everyone.

■ Contribute to the success of young people in the world of work, and to their personal development and fulfilment.

■ Support the achievement of the new National Targets for Education and Training with their aim of providing a national workforce able to meet the international competitive challenge through high levels of skill and adaptability to change.

1.6   I presented an Interim Report in July 1995. Ministers endorsed it as the basis for work leading to this Final Report.

1.7   In both stages I have worked closely with Sir Michael Heron, the Chairman of the NCVQ, and Mr Rudi Plaut, the Chairman of the Curriculum and Assessment Authority for Wales (ACAC). We have been supported by a team drawn from the Department for Education and Employment, the National Council for Vocational Qualifications, the School Curriculum and Assessment Authority and the Further Education Development Agency. The names of the team members are listed below. We record our thanks to them.

Geoff Lucas (Team Leader)   Caroline Mager
Patricia Bellas   Paul Man
Chris Boys   Tony Millns
Nancy Braithwaite   Nicola Napier
Paul Coates   Julie Sohal
Shaila Hussein   Madeleine Swords

1.8   We are grateful to our consultation group and to the many people who contributed to this Review.

Terms

1.9   It has been impossible to write this Report without constant reference to a host of qualifications and bodies of one kind or another, all with impressively long titles. To avoid the text being dominated by long recitals of names, extensive use of initials has been necessary. The reader is advised to refer to the list of abbreviations at the back of this Report.

1.10 To assist the reader four collective nouns have been used.

Government departments	Department for Education and Employment, the Welsh Office and the Northern Ireland Office
regulatory bodies	National Council for Vocational Qualifications (NCVQ); School Curriculum and Assessment Authority (SCAA); Curriculum and Assessment Authority for Wales (ACAC) and Council for the Curriculum, Examinations and Assessment (Northern Ireland) (CCEA), which set or approve national standards, and monitor the quality assurance and assessment arrangements of awarding bodies to ensure that they work fairly and effectively.
awarding bodies	The bodies which make awards such as the GCSE, A levels, the GNVQ and NVQ.
key skills	Skills in communication, the application of number and information technology.

Introduction

1.11 This Report proposes a coherent national framework covering all the main qualifications and the achievements of young people at every level of ability. It goes beyond that, to recognise achievement outside the main formal qualifications, as part of a restructured and relaunched National Record of Achievement. Because the qualifications appropriate for 16–19 year olds are relevant to people of all ages, it takes into account the needs of adults, particularly those studying part-time. It identifies barriers to achievement and ways to deal with them.

1.12 Stability is important, so the proposed national framework is based on the present qualifications. But it seeks to bring the structure of A levels and the General National Vocational Qualification (GNVQ) into close alignment. This is to enable students to build up a portfolio of qualifications across both pathways. It proposes the renaming of the Advanced GNVQ as the 'Applied A level'.

1.13 The Report argues that the structure of bodies for regulating and making awards should reflect the recent merger of the Government's responsibilities for education and training into the Department for Education and Employment. This will help to bring greater coherence into the framework of qualifications and challenge pervasive attitudes inherited from the past towards the relative worth of achievement in the academic and vocational pathways.

1.14 The Report responds to the representations by employers on the need to build up competence in the key skills of communication, the application of number and information technology, as well as to their concerns to see young people develop wider skills such as team-working, problem-solving and managing their own learning.

1.15 It gives explicit recognition and support through the qualifications system to the National Targets for Education and Training.

1.16 Following the report of the National Commission on Education, it also encourages an option for post-16 education that combines depth of study with breadth. A high level of achievement in communication, the application of number and information technology is a precondition of the proposed award.

1.17 The Report proposes a new approach to Youth Training and its relaunch with a new national identity.

1.18 It addresses concerns about the rigour of A levels, and welcomes the proposals to improve GNVQs and NVQs, made in the Capey and Beaumont reviews, with which I co-operated during the work leading to this Report.

1.19 The Report gives support to the development of a strengthened GNVQ as a major alternative to A levels and as a means of providing the underpinning knowledge and understanding for broad occupational areas and progression to NVQs. It seeks to encourage young people across the whole ability range to consider the options now available for combining work with part-time study for NVQ qualifications from the age of 16.

1.20 Through a range of proposals, including a new Advanced Subsidiary qualification, the restructuring of the GNVQ, and high-quality advice to young people on the choices they have to make, it seeks to reduce the present levels of non-completion and wastage in post-16 education. These proposals seek thereby to help learners get recognition for their achievements, and to secure more effective use of public resources.

1.21 While the Report is primarily concerned with those aged between 16 and 19, in proposing the recognition of achievement below the GCSE, and with those with learning difficulties particularly in mind, it also extends to 14–16 year olds.

1.22 The Report makes proposals that are often capable of adoption in the next two to three years, so that an early response can be made to issues arising from the fast expansion of post-16 education and training. At the same time, the underpinning structure envisaged in the proposals is capable of further development and adaptation in the longer term, should that be appropriate.

1.23 Finally, and most importantly, the achievements in education and training to which we aspire, and the developments proposed in this Report, can only be realised through teachers, lecturers and trainers, and with their active support. My recommendations have important implications for the approach to learning and for teacher training and development; they assume that the potential of information and communications technology for enhancing the range, effectiveness and quality of teaching will continue to be harnessed. These issues will need particular attention in the action that follows this Report.

SECTION 2

Summary of views expressed in evidence to the Review

2.1 Between July 1995, when the Interim Report was published, and the beginning of 1996, an extensive programme of meetings, conferences, and consultation took place. Details of this programme, and a full summary of the views expressed in evidence to the Review, are given in Appendix A. This section provides a snapshot of the views of employers, students, schools, colleges and universities, drawing on views expressed and the research undertaken for the Review. (See Appendix B.)

The views of employers

2.2 In summary, employers:

■ Respect the established General Certificate of Secondary Education (GCSE) and Advanced (A) levels, but are looking for more than they provide.

■ Have as yet little knowledge of General National Vocational Qualifications (GNVQs) and reserve judgement on them, but welcome the provision they make for developing some general competences valued in the workplace.

■ Have a strong commitment to the concept of a family of employment-based qualifications designed and owned by industry, as provided by National Vocational Qualifications (NVQs), but want changes in this.

■ Have strong concerns about levels of general skills in particular, standards in oral and written communication and numeracy.

The barriers of complexity and change

2.3 The general mass of employers, and especially the small to medium sized employers who form the great majority, are bewildered by the present range of qualifications. They want stability and simplicity in the framework.

2.4 It takes about ten years for a qualification to become generally known. Industry and commerce have too many other pressing demands on their attention for managers, especially line managers, to keep abreast of educational developments. Even the GCSE, which has been in existence for seven years, is still often referred to as O levels. Only A levels, with 45 years behind them, are common currency. That fact, and the qualities they are seen to represent, are important reasons for their high standing.

2.5 By contrast, the GNVQ is little known, except by name. This is not surprising since it began to produce qualifications only three years ago. The NVQ, which was introduced nine years ago, is well established in many sectors of industry, and even where it has made only modest headway it is generally known. But understanding of it, and therefore its take-up, has been limited by the complexity of structures and language surrounding it.

2.6 Unless we can bring greater simplicity, everyday English and stability into the system of qualifications, employers will not be helped to make good decisions in recruitment. Their commitment to training will be blunted, and they will tend to play for safety by recruiting on the basis of the qualifications they know best. But the national interest will not be best served by the indefinite expansion of the well-known A levels. They were designed for a particular purpose, and neither motivate nor lend themselves to access by all.

Standards in communication and the application of number

2.7 As demonstrated in Section 7 representations by employers about standards in communication and the application of number have been a feature of national life for more than a century. It has always seemed that things were better twenty years ago.

2.8 Such complaints are still with us, from small firms and large ones, both in industry and in commerce. They come equally from bodies representing employers including the Association of British Chambers of Commerce, the Confederation of British Industry and the Institute of Directors. Employers want entrants with a good command of language, both oral and written, and also a good grasp of basic arithmetic without the help of a calculator. The higher the level of recruit, the more that is expected.

2.9 The issue that came across again and again from employers was the concern to see better standards in these two key skills.

Information Technology

2.10 One of the encouraging features of the consultation was the near-absence of any representation from employers about the familiarity of entrants to work with information technology. This reflects the extent of commitment given by education to the use of information technology, where the United Kingdom has been in advance of many other countries. It is much to the credit of our schools and colleges.

Other core skills

2.11 Employers are looking to education to respond to their wish to see entrants to employment possessing or developing a range of skills that are valued highly in all forms of work. These include:

- Personal and inter-personal skills, in particular, effectiveness in working as a member of a team.

- The ability to manage one's own learning, as a skill needed for life-long learning.

- A positive problem-solving approach.

The views of students

2.12 The majority of students felt that there was a big jump between their GCSEs and their current courses. This was most marked for A level students, nearly all of whom made this point. Some claimed that they had been insufficiently prepared by the GCSE.

2.13 Most students also commented on their increased workloads. A proportion of GNVQ students post-16 were found to be taking the first year to upgrade their GCSE or to obtain an Intermediate GNVQ before moving on to a two-year course for the Advanced GNVQ. Most who had chosen the GNVQ found the approach to study rewarding and motivating. This was less noticeable, however, with the required development of skills in communication, the application of number and information technology, where many institutions are still developing approaches to integrate the acquisition of these skills into the main studies.

Choice of course

2.14 There was little difference between students taking different qualifications in the sources of advice that they drew on to make decisions about which courses to take. 'Official' channels – teachers and careers officers – tended to be more important than informal advice from parents, friends, or other students. Students were reasonably positive about their contact with careers staff. But they did stress the importance of high-quality, independent advice.

2.15 On the issue of breadth as opposed to depth of education, students appeared to be content with the close focus of A levels, while International Baccalaureate students were content with the breadth offered by their qualification. The International Baccalaureate is however available in only a small proportion of schools and colleges. A level students are primarily interested in meeting the requirements for university entrance, for which the present pattern of a narrow range of subjects is well established.

2.16 On reflection some A level students regretted having to make choices about subject options, courses and qualifications before 16. They felt that they were too young to make decisions which were likely to bear so much on their future. Some students felt that their choice of degree had been restricted by the narrow range of A levels, and would have preferred a broader range of subjects at 16.

2.17 GNVQ students were concerned about the acceptability of their qualification to both higher education and employers. A level students had no such misgivings. As a result, one strategy was for GNVQ students intending to seek a university place to take an A level alongside the GNVQ at Advanced level. Once in higher education, students who had followed GNVQ courses felt that they were on a par with A level students in gaining the necessary background knowledge required for tackling their chosen course in higher education.

2.18 It was noticeable that A level students who had moved straight into employment felt that they were less prepared for it than their GNVQ peers. They had two main concerns. They felt that A level students who entered work rather than higher education were not given enough support or assistance by their schools or colleges. They particularly lacked experience of group work, presentational skills, and information technology.

Attitudes of 16–19 year olds to skills valued by employers

2.19 An enquiry conducted amongst 16–19 year olds (see Appendix B4) provided the following insights.

- ■ A strong consensus that skills in communication and working with others were very important to 16–19 year olds.

■ A smaller but still substantial majority of students felt that information technology and the application of number were very important. Less than half felt that problem-solving was very important, and only a minority felt that foreign languages were necessary.

■ While there were subject and qualification differences, the majority of respondents felt that they were developing a wide range of skills irrespective of the type of course they were taking. Differences reflected the nature of qualifications or subjects chosen by young people.

■ GNVQ respondents gave a particularly favourable rating to the growth in skills in working with computers, working in groups, and giving presentations. There was little difference between GNVQ and A/AS ratings of improvements being achieved in working under pressure, written expression, and understanding written information.

Views on assessment

2.20 Few students, whatever the type of qualification, felt that final examinations alone assessed knowledge and understanding fairly or reflected ability accurately. Neither was there a great deal of support for assessment to be exclusively conducted through course work. There was no consensus about alternatives to final examinations, although the most widely supported form of assessment was a mixture of modular exams and course work. Support for this mixed form of assessment came from both A level and GNVQ students.

The views of schools and colleges

2.21 Latest indications are that approximately 30 per cent of students in Further Education lack the skills in basic literacy and numeracy to benefit fully from their courses[1]. Further education colleges continue to express their concern.

2.22 While schools are increasingly attracted to introducing applied and vocational education, mainly in the form of GNVQs, and are supportive of the concept, most of them are newcomers to this field. Where schools – especially those with smaller sixth forms – are introducing GNVQs, they have concerns about the practicalities of implementation, relating in particular to funding and resources, guidance, training and the clarity of specifications. Although the GNVQ has been welcomed, institutions have criticised the complexity of its structure and the heavy burden of assessment.

2.23 Both schools and colleges are concerned about the dominance of A levels in the minds of parents, students and universities, and the extent to which this can affect decisions on courses to the detriment of the long-term interest of students. There is a widely-shared wish to see qualifications develop in a way that will redress the balance between the esteem of A levels and of the GNVQ and the NVQ. Schools and colleges very much want the GNVQ to achieve high acceptability and use as an excellent pathway for harnessing the enthusiasm and abilities of many students who are attracted by the subject content, its relevance to careers, and its distinctive approach to learning.

2.24 The general availability of A levels in modular form has been widely welcomed by the awarding bodies and by institutions. This is welcomed in its own right, and as providing a potential basis for combining A level and GNVQ studies.

---

[1] Source: the Basic Skills Agency (1996).

2.25 Many in the further education sector would welcome a fully unitised system of qualifications allowing for credit accumulation and transfer. They see the added flexibility that this would offer as particularly relevant to adult learners. They also see it as helping to improve motivation and a sense of achievement.

2.26 There is concern to recognise all achievement across the whole range of ability. Institutions want to be able to respond effectively to those who are not succeeding at school. They are looking for new approaches which will kindle interest and enthusiasm. This is seen as a key to achievement, and recognition of earned achievement is seen as a powerful motivator. Schools are particularly concerned about young people of compulsory school age who are failing to attend school, are demotivated and not achieving their potential. Colleges find that an increasing proportion of their intake consists of young people who have not achieved much, if anything, at school. Providing appropriate (and often remedial) education and training for them is a priority for many colleges.

2.27 For those with outstanding ability, schools see advantage in a broadening experience as an alternative to further study in a chosen specialism. There is concern to encourage and recognise achievement beyond A levels and GNVQs.

2.28 The National Record of Achievement has wide support, but there is disappointment that it has not achieved as much as was hoped in terms of being seen by universities and employers as relevant to their recruitment processes.

2.29 There are many representations about funding methodologies, which are seen as affecting student choice and reducing desirable co-operation between institutions.

2.30 Finally, there is clear recognition of the importance of high-quality independent advice and guidance to students in making decisions from the age of 14 onwards on choice of course, institution and potential career. This is seen as relevant not only in reducing wastage from courses, but in ensuring that students are guided to the institutions that are likely to serve them best. (Appendix C1 shows the participation of 16, 17 and 18 year olds in education and training, where they are and the courses that they take.)

The views of universities

2.31 The universities share the wish of employers to see entrants coming to them with higher standards in communication and the application of number. It is becoming increasingly common practice for universities to offer special courses to enable undergraduates to improve their skills in these areas. On this issue the universities are united. On the use of information technology, universities generally acknowledge that performance is getting better year by year, and that given the opportunity, students are willing to remedy any deficiencies of their own accord.

2.32 There is strong support for maintaining the rigour of A levels. A particular point of concern is the standard in mathematics among those presenting themselves for degree courses in that subject, and in the physical sciences. Universities are saying that unless standards can be improved it may be necessary to move to a four-year degree course. There are also some concerns to see those coming forward to read for degrees in modern foreign languages having a stronger grounding in the syntax and grammar of the languages to be studied.

2.33 Especially among the newer universities, which have well-developed modular degree courses, modular A levels are seen as compatible with their own systems. They consider that students who have followed modular courses are better able to manage their own learning. But some of the older universities question whether modular A levels are the best preparation for higher education, for example in terms of undertaking long assignments and developing essay writing skills.

2.34 Views on the value of Special Papers for the ablest A level students vary. Some welcome these and wish them to be continued. Others have doubts about the value of extended study of a subject in depth, and see greater benefit for many students in broadening their experience, whether through a wider range of studies or the kind of development that comes from work in the community, the Duke of Edinburgh's Award Scheme, Young Enterprise and similar activities. In making choices between students who have similar A level attainments, universities are often looking for that something extra which shows character, distinctiveness or enterprise on the part of the student. As a broadening experience there were expressions of some interest in the kind of experience provided through the International Baccalaureate, which would give able students from different disciplines an opportunity to explore the various forms of knowledge, so that they develop a rigorous and logical approach which could inform their work as undergraduates.

2.35 As yet the universities have too little experience of the GNVQ to reach any firm conclusions. But the comment was made that the GNVQ awards system should be more finely tuned than pass, merit and distinction. There was also some comment that the GNVQ forms of assessment might not fully prepare students for tasks in higher education such as note-taking and extended essay writing.

2.36 The universities supported the proposals of the Higginson Committee in 1988 for broadening the studies between 16 and 19 to cover five subjects rather than the typical three A levels. The universities continue to support a broader basis for post-16 study, and while decisions on admissions remain with admissions tutors, vice-chancellors consider that the approach recommended by the National Commission on Education would be welcome as one of the options that should be available. They were interested by a particular formulation put to them for consideration, based upon studies covering four named areas of study (science, technology, engineering and mathematics; the arts and humanities; a modern foreign language; 'the way the community works', including business, economics, government and politics, law, psychology and sociology). This would involve two A levels, or the equivalent in the applied and vocational pathways, and studies equal to the new AS covering other areas, plus achievement of a good standard in communication, the application of number and information technology.

S E C T I O N 3

A national framework of qualifications

The framework of qualifications

3.1 The range of qualifications for 16–19 year olds is vast. There are at least 16,000. This reflects the wide range of purposes they are designed to serve, the multiplicity of awarding bodies, and the simultaneous availability of qualifications being phased in while others are phased out.

3.2 What we have is the product of history. Initiatives have followed one another over time. Each has been designed for its own purpose, with limited concern to provide coherence and ready understanding on the part of students, parents and employers, or to provide a framework in which it is possible to combine elements from different pathways, or to move from one pathway to related study in another.

3.3 The consultations undertaken for this Review have brought home the problem that those of us concerned with the provision of qualifications have created for others. It is all too easy for those professionally engaged in the central administration of qualifications to over-estimate the level of knowledge about the present maze of qualifications among parents and small and medium sized employers. Even those engaged in education sometimes need help.

3.4 The very names of the qualifications seem perversely selected to provide a barrier to memory and understanding: the GCSE; GCE A level; GNVQ and NVQ, as they are called. The full titles are even less memorable.

3.5 Some employers consulted still think of the General Certificate of Secondary Education (GCSE), introduced eight years ago, as the O level it superseded. Few outside education know more than the name of the General National Vocational Qualification (GNVQ). The National Vocational Qualification (NVQ), which has been available for some nine years, is a familiar term in major industries. But the complexity of the systems associated with it has been a major barrier to involvement and understanding among small companies. Only the A level, for which the prefix 'GCE' has been happily dropped by all but the cognoscenti, is a common currency, thanks largely to the 45 years it has had to establish itself. This long life, and its innate quality, have earned the A level its designation as the so-called 'gold standard'. But the standing of A levels has led to their expansion beyond the purposes for which they were created. Their further expansion would most probably serve to increase the already too high proportion of disappointed students who find the A level approach is not right for them. (See Appendix B1 and B2.)

3.6 Employers, parents, students, apprentices, trainees, and careers advisers need to make well-informed judgements on courses and qualifications. The framework of qualifications as a whole needs to be one that helps them to do so. Its design should facilitate understanding, progression within and between qualifications pathways, economy in teaching, recognition of all achievement, and the building up of a portfolio of qualifications from different pathways whose collective weight can be readily appraised. We need a common vocabulary of terms, free from the present technical jargon.

3.7 This Review has given an opportunity to address these issues, and in doing so to make explicit the equal standing of academic, applied and vocational qualifications. This can be achieved without creating a new turmoil of change, by grouping the present qualifications in the three main pathways into three levels, and introducing a fourth level to recognise achievement by those who find progress in education and training most difficult.

3.8 I **recommend** that these four levels should be known as

Advanced
Intermediate
Foundation
Entry

3.9 I also **recommend** that they should be known as **National Levels,** and that the term **National** should be the term that characterises all the main elements in the framework envisaged in the Report[1]. These include:

National Awards
National Record of Achievement
National Traineeships
National Certificates
National Advanced Diploma
National Vocational Qualifications

3.10 This will signify the national backing and recognition given to achievement of all kinds that meets national standards. The proposals made in the Report are designed to relate to the National Targets for Education and Training[2]. It adopts the equivalences of achievement used in the three main qualifications pathways in the National Targets, while recognising that these may need reassessment in the light of experience. The National Targets are:

■ By age 19, 85 per cent of young people to achieve five GCSEs at grade C or above, an Intermediate GNVQ or a full NVQ level 2.

■ 75 per cent of young people to achieve level 2 competence in communication, numeracy and information technology by age 19; and 35 per cent to achieve level 3 competence in these skills by age 21.

■ By age 21, 60 per cent of young people to achieve 2 A levels, an Advanced GNVQ or a full NVQ level 3.

---

[1] It is for consideration to what extent in Wales these should be identified as 'Welsh National'.

[2] In Wales there is also a distinctive target for achievement in the core subjects by 15 year olds under the *Bright Future* programme.

Table 1 Proposed framework of national awards

National Award: Advanced Level

AS and A Level	GNVQ Advanced Level	NVQ Level 3†

National Award: Intermediate Level

GCSE Grades A*-C	GNVQ Intermediate Level	NVQ Level 2‡

National Award: Foundation Level

GCSE Grades D-G	GNVQ Foundation Level	NVQ Level 1‡

National Award: Entry Level*

Common to all pathways:
Three grades A/B/C

---

† NVQ Level 3 obtained by young people primarily through a Modern Apprenticeship/Employment.

‡ NVQ Levels 1 and 2 obtained by young people primarily through Youth Training/Employment.

* Entry Level at grades A, B, C equivalent in demand to Levels 3, 2 and 1 of the National Curriculum, but contextualised for the post-16 age group.

13

3.11 The qualifications would be grouped into four proposed nationally recognised levels of achievement; Table 1 outlines a proposed framework of National Awards for 16–19 year olds, which would also apply to other learners.

3.12 The qualifications ranking for the two higher levels are based on the levels in the National Targets for Education and Training. Awards, other than the A level, the GCSE, the GNVQ and NVQ, which need to be recognised for a National Award at these levels should be considered by the regulatory bodies for inclusion on the basis of strict criteria. The proposed Entry level is not covered either by the National Targets or by national qualifications. Section 12 of this Report includes proposals for the Entry level.

3.13 I recommend that:

■ All certificates issued by awarding bodies should show the relevant national level prominently as the main heading. To assist understanding of what has been achieved, the new certificates should include (on the reverse side) a list of the main comparable nationally recognised achievements at the relevant level. The face of the certificate should give more detail than at present about the nature of the achievement. For certificates at the Advanced level, provision should be made for including the numerical score based on the Universities and Colleges Admissions Service (UCAS) proposed new tariff. A certificate number should be included on each certificate.

■ National criteria should be developed in order to recognise and formally ascribe national levels to other current major qualifications which fall outside the three main qualifications pathways.

■ The form of the new certificates would be as illustrated in Appendices C2-C5 and at the end of this Section.

3.14 The proposed national framework for awards, besides enabling everyone to understand the levels of the various qualifications, has the important purpose of making plain that academic, applied and vocational qualifications are of equal value. Recent developments in the qualifications framework in Scotland, which are designed to achieve similar objectives, are given in Appendix D.

Clarity of purpose for the three main pathways

3.15 If the framework of qualifications is to be intelligible to students, parents, employers and employees, we need to make explicit the essential purposes and characteristics of each of the three main qualifications pathways.

3.16 There is no problem about this with the NVQ: it is a qualification designed by industry and commerce specifically to mark competence in a particular trade or profession. The problem comes at the interface between A levels and the GNVQ. Both are designed to be taught in schools and colleges, and many people, prospective employers for instance, may be perplexed when they find that there is an A level in business studies and an Advanced GNVQ in business, an A level in art and an Advanced GNVQ in art and design, and an A level in science and an Advanced GNVQ in science. Without knowing the detail of the courses, it is difficult for people to understand the difference.

3.17 It would help everyone if there was to be a consistent distinctiveness between the A level and the GNVQ at the Advanced level, and also between the GCSE on the one hand and the GNVQ at the Intermediate and Foundation levels on the other.

3.18 No discussion of the distinctiveness of the GCSE and A level pathway can take place without recognising that learning at schools and colleges is much concerned with things that have very practical purposes. Learning to speak and write effectively, to count and know about the world, are practical needs. There is nothing fundamentally academic about them. Over the years, the practice has developed of assessing and recognising achievement up to the age of 16 in the subjects taught in schools through the GCSE. Indeed, when the GCSE was launched, the Government leaflet describing it referred to it as including practical learning. I see no reason to change the present general practice of using the GCSE to make assessments for subjects covered by the National Curriculum, for religious education, or for subjects that have historically been regarded as part of an academic curriculum. But now that we have the GNVQ at the Foundation and Intermediate levels, there is a strong case for seeing subject areas like leisure and tourism, or health and social care, as being the province of the GNVQ.

3.19 At A level, the issue becomes more pertinent because the GNVQ was essentially designed as a qualification for those over 16.

3.20 To many, A level is associated with the academic study of a subject or discipline, and its links with other areas of knowledge and experience. Such disciplines are often defined as having a tradition and a canon; they tend to be self-standing (with their own methods and approaches); and they are associated with the development of cognitive breadth, higher level skills of analysis, synthesis and critical evaluation and the pursuit of a subject for its own interest.

3.21 In recent years, however, many A levels have broadened their range and appeal by stressing the relevance of the knowledge, understanding and skills they seek to develop. Some, particularly those involving more practical subjects, have emphasised the applied nature of much of their content.

3.22 There are two bases for making a distinction between the GCSE and A level on the one hand and the GNVQ on the other. They are, first, the purpose of the associated course of study, and second, the style of learning and assessment. In fact the two are clearly associated, because the style of learning and assessment should be derived from and serve the purpose of the course.

3.23 Such distinctions cannot be sharply defined. There will be features common to both pathways, and a blurred frontier. There are also personal factors which will influence delivery of qualifications in both pathways, such as individual teacher and student approaches to learning. But at the core, and in the main approach, there should be distinctiveness.

3.24 I **recommend** that the distinguishing characteristics appropriate to each pathway should reflect the underlying purpose, as outlined below.

A Level and GCSE

■ Where the primary purpose is to develop knowledge, understanding and skills associated with a subject or discipline.

Applied Education (GNVQ)

■ Where the primary purpose is to develop and apply knowledge, understanding and skills relevant to broad areas of employment.

Vocational Training (NVQ)

■ Where the primary purpose is to develop and recognise mastery of a trade or profession at the relevant level.

3.25 In making the distinction between GCSE/A levels and the GNVQ, it is also helpful to look at the defining characteristics of the GNVQ family as a whole. These are:

■ Theory, knowledge and skills relevant to a broad area of work.

■ A chance to learn in a practical way by combining classroom and workplace experience.

■ Opportunities for working with others and planning one's own study.

■ General education through the assessment of the key skills in communication, the application of number and information technology.

■ Vocational units which provide general education in a vocational context.

■ Enhancing employment prospects while also providing for access to higher education.

3.26 I **recommend** that below A level, it should be accepted that the GCSE develops general education as well as the practical application of skills, for example in communication and the application of number. But in subject areas outside the National Curriculum, or where GCSE subject-specific criteria do not already exist, studies in the practical applications of knowledge and understanding relevant to broad areas of employment should normally be regarded as the province of the GNVQ, unless there are good reasons to the contrary.

3.27 The practical interpretation of such principles needs to be settled by the regulatory bodies, subject to the approval of the Secretaries of State, and in consultation with the awarding bodies. I therefore **recommend** that:

■ The joint committee of the NCVQ and SCAA outlined in Section 4 should enter into discussion with the awarding bodies and recommend broad principles for allocating subject areas to pathways, for the approval of the Secretaries of State.

■ The joint committee should consider all proposals for new awards and programmes, and make recommendations to the parent bodies. As qualifications come forward for revision and approval, their appropriateness for a particular pathway should be reviewed.

■ The joint committee might also consider whether in the longer term there is a case for a national subject framework for qualifications based on coherent groupings of broad subject areas.

3.28 Arrangements have been made for Wales and Northern Ireland to take part in this work.

Transfer between pathways

3.29 The case has been made in the preceding paragraphs for distinctiveness between the 'academic' and 'applied' pathways.

3.30 But with the prospect that both pathways will be available in most institutions teaching 14–19 year olds, some students will be interested in the possibility of building up a portfolio of qualifications that includes qualifications from both pathways. Others may wish to move between pathways, if in the light of experience they conclude that they have made the wrong choice or that they could make a better choice.

3.31 The increasing availability of A levels in modular form, and the way the GNVQ has been structured in units from the outset, suggest that where an A level and a GNVQ cover similar areas of knowledge and understanding, some transferring between pathways may be feasible. The possibility that the student might wish to make a transfer, even though the content of the A level and the GNVQ may have a good deal in common, arises from the different learning and assessment styles that characterise the two qualifications, and their different purposes.

3.32 Before this Review was commissioned, the Gatsby Foundation had proposed a study of the potential for identifying common content. The Review team has collaborated with the Foundation on this. Appendix B5 summarises the findings.

3.33 The study has been concerned with two distinct but related issues.

- Whether common content can be identified, and whether transfer from one pathway to the other is possible.

- Whether it is feasible for students on A level and GNVQ courses to cover common content together and, if they did so, whether they would learn enough about the distinctiveness of each pathway to make an informed choice of which would suit them better.

3.34 The Gatsby study has shown that there is some demand for transfer between pathways, but from A level to GNVQ rather than vice-versa.

3.35 The study has also shown that there is sufficient common content in some subject areas to open up the possibility of one common unit, for about one term's work. To go beyond this would mean looking again at the content of courses. The study also suggests that it would be possible to teach A level and GNVQ students together during this period, but this would involve difficulties arising from the different design of A levels and GNVQs. More might be possible if the common content of A level and GNVQ courses were increased.

3.36 It would be wrong, however, to seek to build up common elements if this were to undermine the distinctive purposes being served by an A level or a GNVQ.

3.37 I **recommend** that in the light of the outcome of the Gatsby project, awarding bodies should examine the scope for identifying common content in related areas of study in modular A levels and GNVQs, bearing in mind the feasibility of common elements being taught together, but without changing the distinctive nature and rigour of each of these qualifications.

Towards a common timetable and common arrangements for quality assurance

3.38 In the interests of students, parents, higher education, employers and the general public, national qualifications are subject to the quality assurance arrangements of the regulatory bodies.

3.39 These arrangements govern the development and approval of qualifications and syllabuses, the timetables for development and approval, arrangements for centre approval[2], and requirements for assessment, recording, grading and the moderation of standards.

3.40 However, different arrangements currently apply to GCSEs, A levels, GNVQs, NVQs and other qualifications. This naturally raises questions as to why this should be so, and whether qualifications are monitored with equal rigour in each system.

3.41 Previous paragraphs have outlined proposals for a national framework of qualifications, and later sections will consider how the rigour of these individual qualifications may be enhanced.

3.42 In a coherent national framework it is necessary to develop a securely-based system of quality assurance which applies equally to all national qualifications. Progress to that end will underline the value and status of all qualifications. This is a consideration that matters to young people. (See Appendix B4 for a summary of a research project on young people's perceptions of these issues.)

3.43 Such quality assurance arrangements will need to recognise the distinctive characteristics of qualifications and avoid compromising them. But there is much to be gained from co-ordinating work across the binary line that divides GCSE and A levels from GNVQs and NVQs, a key characteristic of our present arrangements. I **recommend** that:

- ■ The joint committee of the NCVQ and SCAA should, in consultation with centres, awarding bodies and representatives of higher education and employment, oversee the development of a common framework for the quality assurance of all national qualifications.

- ■ The committee should take into account the extent to which a common framework might recognise the distinctive features of qualifications and avoid compromising them.

- ■ These arrangements should include common timetables for the review, development and approval of qualifications in related subject areas.

- ■ These arrangements should cover the development and approval of syllabuses, the roles of centres, awarding and regulatory bodies in assessment, recording, grading, moderation, monitoring, and centre approval.

Centre approval relates to the steps taken by an awarding body to ensure that a centre is able to carry out its role in the assessment of particular awards. In NVQs and GNVQs, centre approval forms part of the verification process through which awarding bodies monitor the performance of centres.

- Awarding bodies should be encouraged to revise codes of practice in the light of the common quality assurance framework.

- Particular attention should be paid to how these arrangements might apply to the development and approval of NVQs and work-based training such as Modern Apprenticeships, and the new initiatives to replace Youth Training which are proposed in Section 5.

- In developing its proposals, the joint committee should consider ways of increasing the cost-effectiveness and reducing the workload in schools and colleges.

The proposed new UCAS profile and qualifications tariff

3.44 During the Review, the Universities and Colleges Admissions Service (UCAS) was consulted about various proposals in the context of its work on a new profile and tariff to replace the current 'points system' for entry to higher education and employment. The present system, originally developed by the Universities Central Council on Admissions (UCCA), is no longer considered adequate. The scoring system is seen by many as arbitrary, it does not show achievement in the different aspects of a student's overall profile, and breadth is not distinguished from depth. The work being undertaken by UCAS (summarised in Appendix F3) will provide a means of recognising and rewarding achievement across the qualifications pathways which is wholly supportive of recommendations made elsewhere in the Report. Appendices F4 and F5 have been provided by UCAS to illustrate the possible form of a UCAS matrix for the National Advanced Diploma proposed in Section 8.

The thickets of complexity and jargon

3.45 All professions have their specialised terms to meet their particular needs, and their distinctive abbreviations and acronyms to save words. But when the specialist communicates with the non-specialist, plain words are needed.

3.46 A distinguishing feature of the world of education and training is its need to communicate on a vast scale every day with non-specialists. It therefore has an exceptionally pressing need to use everyday language which can be understood by every man and woman. Unfortunately the separate development of the different families of qualifications has tended to produce separate specialised vocabularies. The same thing can have different names in different contexts. Complexity abounds.

3.47 I **recommend** that:

- The joint committee of the NCVQ and SCAA should take forward the development of a common vocabulary which should be adopted by the regulatory and awarding bodies for all qualifications.

- The regulatory bodies should commit themselves to using plain words in all their publications.

3.48 I am glad to report that action on the first of these recommendations is already in hand.

National Award: Advanced Level

ABC Awarding Body*

A B Jones has received the following awards at the National Advanced Level:

GNVQ (single award)	Manufacturing	Merit
	Units Awarded†:	
	....	
	....	
AS	Business Studies	Grade B

20 August 1997   No. 1231

Explanatory Note on Awards at the National Advanced Level

National Awards are recognised at four levels:

Advanced

Intermediate

Foundation

Entry

This certificate is an award at the Advanced level

The following are classified as being at the National Advanced Level:

i.	National Vocational Qualification (NVQ)	Level 3
ii.	General National Vocational Qualification (GNVQ)	Advanced level with grades of Distinction, Merit and Pass
	Double Award[1]	
	Single Award[2,3]	
iii.	A level	Grades A, B, C, D and E
	AS[4]	
iv.	Other qualifications recognised as Advanced include ....(to be determined)	

---

[1]   The full GNVQ (12 units plus three key skills units) is referred to in the Report as an Applied A level (Double Award).

[2]   The proposed six unit GNVQ (including three key skills units) is called an Applied A level in the Report, and will be equal in weight to a single A level award.

[3]   At present, there is no formal GNVQ award equivalent to the AS. However, three GNVQ units are equal in weight to the AS.

[4]   An AS (Advanced Subsidiary) is equivalent to half an A level.

National Award: Intermediate Level

ABC Awarding Body*

A B Jones has received the following awards at the National Intermediate Level

GNVQ Intermediate Level	Leisure and Tourism	Merit
	Units Awarded†:	
	....	
	....	
GCSE	Mathematics	Grade B

20 August 1997

No. 1232

---

*   For the purpose of example only.

†   The units would be individually listed.

22

Explanatory Notes on Awards at the National Intermediate Level

National Awards are recognised at four levels:

Advanced

Intermediate

Foundation

Entry

This certificate is an award at the Intermediate Level

The following awards are classified as being at the National Intermediate Level.

i.	National Vocational Qualification (NVQ)	Level 2 achieved by young people through Youth Training/Employment
ii.	General National Vocational Qualification (GNVQ)	Intermediate level with grades of Distinction, Merit and Pass
	Part One GNVQ[1]	
iii.	General Certificate of Secondary Education (GCSE)	Grades A*, A, B and C
	GCSE short course[2]	
iv.	Other qualifications recognised as Intermediate include......................(to be determined)	

---

[1]   A Part One GNVQ (Intermediate Level) is equal in weight to half a full GNVQ or two GCSEs A*–C.

[2]   A GCSE short course is equivalent to half a GCSE.

National Award: Foundation Level

ABC Awarding Body*

A B Jones has received the following awards at the National Foundation Level

Part One GNVQ **Foundation Level**	Leisure and Tourism	Pass
	Units Awarded†:	
	....	
	....	
GCSE	Mathematics	Grade D
	Italian	Grade D

20 August 1997   No. 1233

---

*   For the purpose of example only.

†   The units would be individually listed.

Explanatory Notes on Awards at the National Foundation Level

National Awards are recognised at four levels:

    Advanced

    Intermediate

    Foundation

    Entry

This certificate is an award at the Foundation level

The following awards are classified as being at the National Foundation Level.

i.	National Vocational Qualification (NVQ)	Level 1 achieved by young people through Youth Training/Employment
ii.	General National Vocational Qualification (GNVQ) Part One GNVQ[1]	Foundation level with grades of Distinction, Merit and Pass
iii.	The General Certificate of Secondary Education (GCSE) GCSE short course[2]	Grades D, E, F and G
iv.	Other qualifications recognised as Foundation include.........................(to be determined).	

---

[1]   A Part One GNVQ (Foundation Level) is equal in weight to half a full GNVQ or two GCSEs D–G.

[2]   A GCSE short course is equivalent to half a GCSE.

National Award: Entry Level

ABC Awarding Body

A B Jones has received the following awards at the National Entry Level:

Communication	Grade A
Application of Number	Grade B
Information Technology	Grade A
Personal and Practical Skills	Grade C

20 August 1997

No. 1234

Explanatory Notes on Awards at the National Entry Level

National Awards are recognised at four levels:

Advanced

Intermediate

Foundation

Entry

This certificate is an award at the Entry Level

The following awards are classified as being at the National Entry Level.

plus

either: a list of individual qualifications

or: National Entry Level Awards (Grades A, B and C) offered by ....
(awarding bodies to be determined)

These awards are part of the national framework of qualifications and lead onto GCSE, GNVQ and NVQ awards.

SECTION 4

The regulatory and awarding bodies

Introduction

4.1 This section proposes action to bring together the functions of the National Council for Vocational Qualifications (NCVQ) and School Curriculum and Assessment Authority (SCAA) and considers the implications for Wales and Northern Ireland. It welcomes the initiatives that have recently been taking place to bring together awarding bodies across the binary line that divides the academic from the vocational. It urges further such initiatives. It seeks a marked reduction in the number of bodies awarding National Vocational Qualifications (NVQs).

The facts

4.2 The provision for the regulation and making of awards is complex. Appendices E1 and E2 set out the bodies involved and their roles. The key points are these:

- There are six bodies in England, Wales and Northern Ireland which award the General Certificate of Secondary Education (GCSE) and Advanced (A) levels; three which award General National Vocational Qualifications (GNVQs), and over 100 involved in awarding NVQs.

- The activities of these bodies are overseen by the NCVQ (covering NVQs and GNVQs) and by three bodies – SCAA in England, the Curriculum and Assessment Authority for Wales (ACAC) in Wales and Council for the Curriculum, Examinations and Assessment (CCEA) in Northern Ireland – covering GCSE and A levels.

- In Northern Ireland the same body, the CCEA, is responsible both for the awarding and oversight of GCSE and A levels. In England and Wales these functions are separate, with SCAA and ACAC having responsibility for oversight alone.

- In the present organisational arrangements, there is a binary line dividing 'academic' awards from applied and vocational awards.

- The A level and the GNVQ awarding bodies compete with each other in their respective spheres.

- The three bodies making awards in the GNVQ have exclusive rights to award the GNVQ until 1997; thereafter this will need to be reviewed.

4.3 The present structures give rise to two questions, which are to a degree inter-connected:

- Is it helpful to have so many bodies?

- Is it desirable to have the present division between the 'academic' on the one hand, and the 'applied' and the 'vocational' on the other?

4.4   The academic/vocational divide is widely associated in British attitudes with a division between the able and the less able. The distinction breaks down in the universities, to the extent that degrees preparing undergraduates for the professions, whose work is based on a high level of intellectual achievement, stand high in regard. But until university, the distinction is made. Even though employers press for the provision of applied and vocational qualifications, the old association of A levels with high ability, and the relative unfamiliarity of the GNVQ and even the NVQ, means that employers may 'play safe' in recruitment decisions and hire candidates with A levels.

4.5   This is damaging to the national interest, and to the optimal development of the wide range of talents among young people. It has meant that some have chosen to take A levels which do not suit them, and that industry is under-skilled in two senses: in the sense that the vocations associated with 'making things' have not attracted their full share of talent, and that the British workforce is under-trained in the skills needed for work. The reasons for the decline of British manufacturing industry are doubtless many. But a nation with a system of values that places the vocational skills required in industry and commerce second best is likely to find itself increasingly uncompetitive with other countries that rate these skills more highly.

4.6   The binary line, as a frontier that largely divides the awarding and regulatory bodies, symbolises and enshrines the way we categorise achievement. If that frontier is to be broken, the present binary line should go. The mutual disparagement that sadly sometimes characterises thinking and attitudes in the workplace and in academe needs to be ended.

4.7   I believe that as a national need, organisational structures should not be based on an academic/vocational divide.

The awarding bodies in England, Wales and Northern Ireland

4.8   Turning first to the number of awarding bodies, some competition promotes innovation and responsiveness to customers. Institutions welcome a degree of choice. But competition can lead to an excessive proliferation of awards, as awarding bodies respond to market needs and opportunities, leading to real difficulties in ensuring parity of standards across the whole field. This difficulty applies both within subject areas and across them.

4.9   The present limit of three on the number of bodies awarding the GNVQ comes up for review in 1997. If then the A level bodies were authorised to offer the GNVQ, there could be an increase of six in the number of bodies awarding that qualification. If reciprocally the GNVQ awarding bodies were able to award A levels, the number of A level bodies would increase from six to nine. This would be too many.

4.10 Proceeding from the premise that we need to unify the present binary structure, the best way forward to achieve that, and to avoid a proliferation of provision, is to encourage and facilitate mergers, associations and partnerships across the binary line. During the present Review, I have therefore informally encouraged exploratory discussions to that end. In December 1995, the Business and Technology Education Council and University of London Examinations and Assessment Council announced a merger. In January 1996, the Royal Society of Arts Examinations Board announced that it had formed an association with the University of Cambridge Local Examinations Syndicate. Other discussions have taken place.

4.11 The process of awarding bodies coming together across the binary line should be encouraged by the Government and Government departments, with a view to having joint bodies making awards of the GCSE, A levels and the GNVQ.

- The objective should be to reduce the total number of bodies making awards.

- Except through joint awarding arrangements, no GCSE or A level awarding body should be authorised to award the GNVQ, and none of the three bodies awarding the GNVQ should be authorised to offer A level awards, or to extend the present provision of GCSEs, except in partnership with a body already authorised to make those awards.

4.12 With NVQs, I recognise that the large number of awarding bodies reflects the wide range of occupational sectors, but I doubt whether this complexity benefits employers and candidates. The Government departments should consider ways of encouraging a reduction in the number of bodies (currently over 100) awarding NVQs, while maintaining some diversity and choice within sectors. In particular, the NCVQ and DfEE should examine the number of bodies in those sectors where the certification of NVQs is low. The opportunity should be taken to require more comprehensive information from the bodies awarding NVQs to improve national data on the take-up and achievement of NVQs.

Regulatory bodies in England: the NCVQ and SCAA

4.13 The NCVQ and SCAA are the two main regulatory bodies in England. By way of background information, a note on them is given in Appendix E1.

4.14 The Interim Report indicated a number of possible options for bringing the NCVQ and SCAA into a closer relationship, redistributing their functions, or merging them.

4.15 With the support of the Secretary of State for Education and Employment we have now set up a joint committee[1] of the NCVQ and SCAA with the following terms of reference:

- To make proposals to the NCVQ and SCAA for taking forward the recommendations of the Dearing Review of 16–19 qualifications and related policy matters, and invite the two bodies to implement agreed proposals and, in particular, to:

  - develop joint arrangements agreed by both the NCVQ and SCAA for:

    - the broad strategic oversight of the development of the framework of qualifications;

    - the present coverage and future development of academic and applied qualifications (ie, GCSEs, A levels, and GNVQs);

    - the approval of these qualifications;

    - a common quality assurance framework governing these qualifications.

---

[1]   Wales and Northern Ireland are represented in the work of this joint committee.

    □ develop an agreed common terminology to describe academic and applied qualifications, and where relevant the NVQ.

4.16 Close working between the two authorities has been supported by the Secretary of State appointing each chairman to the other authority, and one member who is common to both. In addition, the two chairmen have supported the work of the Gatsby Foundation to identify common elements in A levels and GNVQ Advanced level courses with a view to providing scope for transfers between programmes and some common teaching. (See Section 3.29–3.37 and Appendix B5.)

4.17 Looking ahead, there are three more fundamental options.

  ■ The first option is:

    □ to transfer responsibility for the GNVQ to SCAA, on the grounds that the GNVQ and A levels will increasingly be taught in the same institutions and the two qualifications are best developed together to provide coherence and complementarity in provision. This would also improve the interface with awarding bodies which offer both qualifications. This transfer could be effected quickly since it would not involve legislation.

  ■ The second and third options, which would require legislation, are:

    □ a full merger of the NCVQ and SCAA;

    □ the creation of two new bodies: a National Qualifications Authority, and another body with responsibility for the school curriculum from 4–19, for national assessment up to the age of 14 and possibly for some other functions presently discharged by other bodies that interface with schools and colleges.

4.18 The first option, a transfer of responsibility for the GNVQ from NCVQ to SCAA, is not recommended for consideration because the GNVQ must be developed with equal regard to complementing the A level in teaching institutions, and to underpinning the NVQ in the workplace. Already there is concern in industry that the GNVQ is not satisfactorily discharging the latter role. It is one which can be confidently assigned only to a body which has a close understanding of the NVQ and employers' interests generally.

4.19 That leaves the second and third options. (Appendix E3 includes a summary of views expressed by representative bodies during the Review on such options.)

4.20 The advantages of a full merger of the NCVQ and SCAA may be summarised as follows:

  ■ It mirrors the merger of the two original sponsoring departments (Education and Employment).

  ■ It gives a serious indication of the Government's commitment to coherence and parity between qualifications, and would facilitate this.

  ■ It places all 'academic', 'applied' and 'vocational' qualifications in the hands of a single body.

■ The interests of employers and vocational concerns might be better reflected in discussions on the school curriculum.

■ It would be well placed to deal with awarding bodies spanning the binary line.

■ Responsibility for curriculum and assessment/public examinations would be kept together.

■ It opens up the NCVQ regional network to the oversight of academic as well as applied and vocational qualifications, with potential for regional in-service training and support.

■ It would mean one fewer non-departmental public body (NDPB) with some longer term economies.

■ It provides a good option for securing an optimum balance between the regulatory approaches of the NCVQ and SCAA, whilst preserving valuable differences.

4.21 The disadvantages of a full merger are:

■ The concentration of power and influence in one body, in an area of key national importance.

■ A risk that the strength of the systems developed over the decades for the academic awards, and the standing they have with the universities, could lead to these approaches superseding those valued by industry.

■ A very demanding role for the chairman/woman and members of the Authority.

■ The risk that to cover all interests adequately, the membership of the controlling body could become large and cumbersome, with an associated loss of effectiveness.

■ The disruptive effect and loss of momentum resulting from a change in organisation.

4.22 Perhaps the key issues relevant to consideration of this option are:

■ The degree of concentration of power for something so central to the country's whole future.

■ Getting the quality of people, able to give the time needed (the chairman/woman would probably need to be full-time).

■ Maintaining the confidence of both the industrial and teaching communities.

4.23 Answers to the concentration of power would have to be found. The Secretary of State could reserve powers to exercise control of key decisions, with the ultimate sanction of terminating the appointments of the board members. As to the loading problem and the maintenance of the confidence of interested parties, much of the work of a merged NCVQ and SCAA would need to be conducted through powerful sub-committees, with, for example, a committee responsible for the NVQ being largely in the hands of people from business and industry; a committee with responsibility for the school curriculum and assessment matters being predominantly drawn from education; and one for public examinations (the GCSE, A levels and GNVQs) with balanced representation.

4.24 These would be valuable safeguards, but the Government would need to be confident of getting the right people, and especially the right full-time chairman/woman, and of the effectiveness of the Secretary of State's reserve powers. Industry and education would need to have confidence in the chairman/woman and the chief executive and in the composition of the board and of its main committees.

4.25 The other option would be to create two new statutory bodies to replace the NCVQ and SCAA:

- A new National Qualifications Authority, covering all nationally recognised awards designed for 14–19 year olds, and all GNVQs and NVQs.

- A new School Curriculum and Assessment Authority for England, responsible for the curriculum in schools from 4–19, and for the national assessment up to the age of 14. Taking advantage of the capacity released by the transfer of some of SCAA's present functions, the body could usefully assume some other functions directly related to the delivery of the school curriculum. Its remit in relation to the 16–19 curriculum in schools would complement the role of the Further Education Development Agency, which supports the education of 16–19 year olds in colleges.

4.26 The advantages and the disadvantages would include many of those outlined as relevant to a full merger, but with two distinctive advantages and one distinctive disadvantage.

4.27 The primary advantage is that it would reduce the concentration of power, and avoid the problem of covering effectively such a wide responsibility through (with the exception of the chairman/woman and chief executive) a part-time board. An important second advantage is that if a National Qualifications Authority were concerned only with national qualifications and not the school curriculum, the employer, school and college communities could feel reassured that their interests were not being subordinated. That would be important to the success of the whole initiative.

4.28 The main disadvantage lies in the creation of an interface problem between the two bodies, which is inescapable short of a complete merger. When, between 1984 and 1993, the responsibility for public examinations for schools was separated from responsibility for the school curriculum, there were serious problems in managing the interface and in ensuring that the requirements laid down for the curriculum matched the wide range of GCSE qualifications which came under the control of a separate body. A secondary disadvantage is that an opportunity to reduce the number of NDPBs may be missed.

4.29 The response to the first disadvantage lies in some cross-membership between the two authorities, including the chairman/woman. As to the second disadvantage, in this context, with so much at stake, it should be a secondary consideration.

4.30 To sum up, I **recommend** that:

- The Government departments should encourage awarding bodies to come together across the binary line to create new joint arrangements for awarding the GCSE, A level and GNVQ.

- The Government departments should, at the same time, take action to rationalise:

  - the number of bodies involved in the awarding of qualifications;

  - the number of NVQ awarding bodies.

- Legislation should be introduced to bring together the work of the NCVQ and SCAA.

- To that end the Government should consult on the following alternatives:

  - bringing together all the work of the NCVQ and SCAA into one single statutory body, or

  - regrouping the qualifications and public examinations functions of the NCVQ and SCAA into a new National Qualifications Authority, with a separate authority responsible for the school curriculum from 4–19, for statutory assessment up to the age of 14, and possibly, in the interests of reducing the number of bodies involved in education, for some other functions.

- The consultation should further consider how employment interests might best be represented in future arrangements in order to ensure that NVQs continue to be based on occupational standards and remain employment-led.

- In the event of legislation, specific provision should be made for Wales and Northern Ireland.

- In the meantime, the Government should support the co-ordinating work of the joint committee of the NCVQ and SCAA, with the full involvement of Wales and Northern Ireland.

Regulatory bodies in Wales and Northern Ireland

4.31 The NCVQ covers Northern Ireland and Wales as well as England. Approval of the GCSE and A levels is the responsibility of ACAC in Wales and of the CCEA in Northern Ireland.

4.32 Thus, if either of the two recommendations above is adopted to bring together existing functions, the resulting body with oversight for qualifications would have a remit covering England for academic awards, and England, Wales and Northern Ireland for applied and vocational awards. The binary divide would still exist in Wales and Northern Ireland where CCEA and ACAC would retain their role of oversight of academic qualifications. I **recommend** that the Welsh Office and the Department for Education in Northern Ireland, together with ACAC, CCEA and their English counterparts, consider which structure would best preserve the responsiveness and distinctiveness of the present arrangements, while progressing towards removing the academic/vocational divide.

4.33 I consider that:

- To extend the roles of ACAC in Wales and of the CCEA in Northern Ireland to cover policy towards, and accreditation of the NVQ would be a major undertaking, and so should not be pursued.

- Recognising the distinctive remits of ACAC and the CCEA as regulatory bodies, and the highly valued role of the WJEC and the CCEA as awarding bodies in responding to distinctive needs in Wales and Northern Ireland, it would be right for ACAC to take on responsibility for the GNVQ framework for Wales and for the CCEA and WJEC to move into awarding GNVQs.

- In the interests of containing the number of bodies making awards, it would however be desirable for WJEC and CCEA, if they wished to be able to offer the whole range of the GNVQs, to do so through association with one of the other awarding bodies. The WJEC has for some years worked closely with City and Guilds, and the CCEA has worked with several vocational awarding bodies. This would avoid the need for them to build up a new body of expertise and administrative arrangements.

- The question of the exercise of the regulatory function for GNVQs in Northern Ireland to reflect local needs will require further consideration.

4.34 Arrangements have already been made for Wales and Northern Ireland representatives to attend meetings of the new joint committee of the NCVQ and SCAA. In the event of the Government deciding on either of the two substantive options discussed in this section for the future of the work of the NCVQ and SCAA, provision would need to be made for representation of Wales and Northern Ireland.

4.35 I **recommend** that:

- The regulatory bodies in Wales and Northern Ireland (ACAC and CCEA) should not extend their roles to cover policy towards and accreditation of the NVQ.

- Further consideration should now be given as a matter of urgency, to ACAC taking responsibility for the GNVQ framework in Wales.

- The CCEA in Northern Ireland and the WJEC in Wales should move into offering GNVQs, through association with one or more of the existing GNVQ awarding bodies.

- Arrangements should be made to provide for Wales and Northern Ireland to take part in the work of any new bodies established to undertake the present work of the NCVQ and SCAA, and meanwhile they will be represented on the joint committee of the NCVQ and SCAA.

SECTION 5

Youth Training and Modern Apprenticeships

Introduction

5.1   The importance of the work-based routes and of the opportunity for work experience, both of which give greater relevance to study for many young people, has been stressed by many respondents to the Review.

5.2   As noted in the Interim Report, there has been a steady decline since 1989 in the proportion of young people involved in employment and training, while participation in full-time post-compulsory study in schools and colleges has grown. However, the *Learning for the Future* report by the University of London Institute of Education and Warwick University envisages that learning in the work-based route will grow in importance. Modern Apprenticeships should support this expansion by raising the status of this way of learning. But to respond fully to national needs, a major expansion requires broader options than Modern Apprenticeships, extending across Youth Training generally.

5.3   The *Learning for the Future* report envisages all learners continuing their development through work-based learning, whether they make the transition from full-time study at 16, at 18+ or after graduating from university. This vision guides the recommendations made here for Youth Training and Modern Apprenticeships which are the two strands of government-funded work-based learning for young people administered by the Training and Enterprise Councils (TECs).

Youth Training

5.4   Youth Training, which was launched in 1990, is a major element in the provision of education and training for 16–19 year olds. The number of young people on Youth Training in Great Britain in September 1995 was 280,000.

5.5   Those taking part in Youth Training aim to achieve National Vocational Qualifications (NVQs) (or their equivalent – SVQs – in Scotland), usually at level 2, over the two years of normal participation. It is available equally to those in jobs, and to the unemployed. There is a guarantee from the Government of an offer of a suitable training place for all 16 and 17 year olds who are not in full-time education or in a job. The allowance gives young people a financial incentive to go into training.

5.6   As the number participating in Youth Training suggests, there has been large-scale take-up. It provides a work-based opportunity to develop skills, and gives recognition of achievement through the NVQ, a qualification designed by industry for industry.

5.7   The government guarantee of a training place to any young person not in full-time education or employment is an excellent investment, and far better in national terms than unconstructive unemployment. But some of those participating are motivated by securing financial benefit from the State rather than by the opportunity to succeed in training. This might be accepted as a cost worth bearing, given the scale of overall benefit from Youth Training, but the involvement of those who have little motivation to achieve affects its whole standing.

5.8 There are also some young people who are not yet ready for NVQ level 1. For these young people Entry level provision is necessary to help them develop their skills and prepare them for progression to NVQs and other qualifications.

5.9 The association of Youth Training with unemployment has unfortunately affected attitudes towards it, its status, and the qualifications associated with it.

5.10 Its standing could be further damaged as more able young people are attracted to places on Modern Apprenticeships (see below). It is also possible that an increasing proportion of those in Youth Training will be young people with special training needs.

5.11 The completion rate for Youth Training is a cause for concern. It is understandable that some young people should leave to take a job, but a completion rate of 46 per cent is unsatisfactory. Although in the period April 1994–January 1995 half of the leavers obtained a full or part qualification, six months after leaving 22 per cent were known to be unemployed.

5.12 A further concern is that Youth Training does not extend the general education of young people. Though NVQs offer appropriate targets for most trainees, many young people would also benefit from opportunities to develop their skills in communication, the application of number and information technology. Although encouraged, this is not a requirement for Youth Training as it is with a Modern Apprenticeship; nor are young people encouraged to take other additional units or full qualifications such as the General National Vocational Qualification (GNVQ) and the General Certificate of Secondary Education (GCSE). More importantly, Youth Training needs to include a formal commitment to regular attendance, punctuality, reliability and personal organisation skills. These are highly valued attributes in every occupation. These practices, which have to be learnt by some, should be inculcated in the training programmes and recognised in the trainees' National Record of Achievement (NRA).

5.13 To sum up, Youth Training is a major part of national provision for education and training. It enables young people to acquire valuable skills and have them recognised through NVQs. But there are problems which need to be addressed. As the *Learning for the Future* report notes, the challenges for Youth Training are to:

■ Maintain its usefulness to employers in meeting level 2 skill needs.

■ Position itself in a continuum promoting progression into Modern Apprenticeships.

■ Maintain momentum at the same time as accommodating entrants with lower educational attainment.

■ Include arrangements for those who are not yet ready for NVQ training.

■ Shed its association with schemes for the unemployed.

5.14 In this context, I **recommend** that:

■ Youth Training[1], however currently named, should be relaunched as a system of **National Traineeships,** available at **Foundation, Intermediate,** and perhaps **Advanced levels,** providing a vocational progression route to Modern Apprenticeships and the work-based route.

■ **National Traineeships** should offer a broad and flexible learning programme for young people, designed by Industry Training Organisations (ITOs) and TECs and delivered in partnership with colleges of further education. Each Traineeship should incorporate NVQs (at levels 1, 2 and perhaps 3 as appropriate to the industry), the three key skills of communication, the application of number and information technology and (where appropriate) other units, short courses and whole qualifications, such as GNVQs and GCSEs.

■ Acceptance to a National Traineeship should be based on an assessment of the applicant's suitability. It should not be the fall-back position for young people without a job.

■ For those not yet ready for NVQ level 1, including those with special training needs and those unclear about their career direction, **National Entry level provision** should be developed, geared towards the Entry level qualifications proposed in this Report (see Section 12), and available through a range of motivating vocational contexts.

■ The National Entry level provision should foster the development of the three key skills of communication, the application of number and information technology including self-expression and handling an interview. This provision would include initial diagnostic assessment of young people's development needs, ongoing guidance and counselling support, and information on careers and training, together with opportunities for work experience and training. Success would be judged by the achievement of the appropriate Entry level qualifications and/or progression into work, training or further education.

■ LEAs, TECs, the Careers Service, schools, colleges and other organisations with experience in developing provision at this level should be involved in developing and managing the National Entry level provision. Opportunities for links with college and school-based initiatives for the Entry level group should be explored, in order to bring coherence locally to education and work-based provision.

■ As with Modern Apprenticeships, applicants for National Traineeships and the National Entry level provision should be required to enter into an agreement with the training provider/TEC, perhaps brokered by the Careers Service, outlining the responsibilities of both the individual and the provider.

■ Clear routes of progression should be established so that young people can readily progress up the levels of the National Traineeship and into Modern Apprenticeships, college-based provision or jobs as appropriate.

---

[1]   Youth Training is known by a multiplicity of names in different TEC areas all over the country.

■ To help young people take full advantage of available progression opportunities and to continue their development, all should receive support in drawing up a career and training plan when they start and when they leave National Traineeships and the National Entry level provision.

■ Quality assurance arrangements for National Traineeships should be developed consistent with those for Modern Apprenticeships. Given the different features of the National Entry level provision, arrangements may differ at this level. All quality assurance arrangements should be closely linked to arrangements in other pathways.

■ Appropriate arrangements should be devised for funding TECs to contribute with local partners to the National Entry level provision.

■ Consideration should be given to reformulating the Government guarantee in the light of proposals for National Traineeships and the National Entry level provision. Decisions on the appropriate provision for any individual should be based on a careful assessment of their training needs.

5.15 Ministers with responsibilities for Wales and Scotland may wish to consider how best to take these matters forward for their young people.

The Modern Apprenticeship

5.16 Modern Apprenticeships were launched nationwide in 1995. They are designed to increase the number of young people achieving level 3 NVQs (or SVQs in Scotland) plus key skills (and in some cases other qualifications and units) in two or three years. Modern Apprenticeships primarily seek to attract able 16 and 17 year olds but are also available to those aged 18, 19 or over.

5.17 Modern Apprenticeships have been developed together by ITOs and TECs. Apprenticeship frameworks have now been approved for over 54 industry sectors, covering two-thirds of the available NVQs at level 3. By the end of 1996, a further 18 are expected to have been approved, thus covering virtually all available NVQs at level 3.

5.18 With transfers from Youth Training, funding for up to 60,000 Modern Apprenticeships is available in 1996–97. This would represent approximately 5 per cent of all 16 and 17 year olds.

5.19 The frameworks that have been developed recognise the importance of developing the key skills (through NCVQ units in communication, the application of number and information technology) that employers expect their young workers to have if they are to progress. Development of these skills is a mandatory requirement in Modern Apprenticeships. This approach is right and links well with proposals for the National Certificates (see Section 8). Those having attained GNVQs in full-time education will be in an excellent position to progress to the relevant Modern Apprenticeship. Those who achieve the NVQ level 3 at 18, 19 or 20 (depending on their age on entry to their Modern Apprenticeship) are at an age where progression through the work-based routes, or through entrance to university diploma or degree courses, will be options.

5.20 In national terms, it would be an advantage for young people who have the potential to rise to senior positions to do so through a variety of routes. This would ensure that there is a range of perceptions and experience in the higher levels of industry and commerce. Learning through work, supported by study, has an advantage over full-time study through the quality of learning that comes from combining the acquisition of knowledge and skills with their application in the workplace. Apprenticeships with good companies, supported by quality training and qualifications, should have high standing.

5.21 Early evaluation of prototype Modern Apprenticeships showed a preponderance of male participation. This may be because the early apprenticeships were in traditional male apprenticeship business sectors. There are also concerns about the level of participation of people from minority ethnic groups. Participation and achievement levels by gender and race should be monitored at national, regional and industry sector levels. The information gained will also be valuable in the context of monitoring achievement of the National Targets through the proposed National Certificates.

5.22 Now that Modern Apprenticeships are nationwide, further consideration might usefully be given to the best balance of involvement of ITOs, awarding bodies and TECs (or LECs in Scotland) in quality assurance. To learn the lessons of early experience, it would be a good investment in the successful development of Modern Apprenticeships to fund the dissemination of good practice through case studies in different occupations and TEC regions.

5.23 I recommend that:

- Schools and the Careers Service should be well briefed so that young people have the Modern Apprenticeship option presented to them.

- Employers should ensure that apprenticeships provide not only the necessary skills, but sufficient underpinning knowledge and understanding to enable Modern Apprentices, having obtained the NVQ level 3, to go on if they wish to part-time, full-time, or sandwich courses leading to diplomas and degrees.

- Progression routes should be defined to make it easier for young people who have attained relevant GNVQs in full-time education to progress to Modern Apprenticeships and NVQs.

- Employers taking on Modern Apprentices should plan their deployment on the completion of the apprenticeship to ensure that momentum is not lost.

- Participation and achievement for males and females, and people from minority ethnic groups, should be monitored at national, regional and industry sector levels.

- Monitoring should be undertaken to identify whether the vocational route is being seen by young people as a means of accessing higher education, and whether qualified apprentices are being offered full- or part-time university places on completion of their Modern Apprenticeships.

- While recognising that the focus lies with 16–17 year olds, there should be research into ways of addressing the balance of provision among 16–25 year olds.

5.24 Ministers with responsibilities for Wales, Scotland and Northern Ireland may wish to consider how best to take these matters forward for their young people.

SECTION 6

The National Record of Achievement

6.1 This Section of the Report is concerned with the role of the National Record of Achievement (NRA) in supporting the framework of qualifications. It records achievement and has potential for further development in helping students to take greater responsibility for their learning and in preparing them to manage their life-long learning as adults.

6.2 At the beginning of this decade, a Director of Nissan UK forecast that by the year 2000, '100 per cent quality' would no longer be a competitive advantage in the market-place for products: it would be merely the entry ticket to it. In the job market, the consultations undertaken for the Review indicate that, four years before the year 2000, formal qualifications now earn an interview but not a job. They are becoming like total quality, an essential entry ticket to the market.

6.3 This is not to detract from the central importance of national qualifications and the work by students and teachers that goes into their achievement. The better the qualification, the better the job that comes within reach. No less important is personal development, in terms of the knowledge, skills and understanding that has been gained. Employers place a high value on formal qualifications, providing they understand them and their worth. That issue of understanding is a major problem in itself, and is dealt with in Section 3 of this Report.

6.4 For university applicants, formal qualifications are often fundamental. Institutions have clear views about the entry standards that they want. But where there is competition for places and applicants' formal qualifications are close to the threshold level, other considerations come to the fore. In these cases, universities are looking for the factor that distinguishes one candidate from another and, having selected that applicant, to be better able to understand what it is they have already achieved and what they are aiming for in the future.

6.5 For this reason, for applicants facing an interview for a job or a university place two issues come into play: what assets besides the formal qualifications they have to offer, and how well they are presented. A comment made particularly by employers is that young people often lack skills in showing to best advantage what they have to offer.

6.6 In both contexts the NRA has a potentially valuable role to play. The NRA was launched in 1991 as a Government-backed initiative. It was intended as a tool for life-long learning and was designed to help individuals plan their future development in education, employment or training. The NRA's greatest success has been in schools: over 80 per cent use the NRA for Year 11 students. Sixteen year olds are presented with an NRA folder as the culmination of a process of reviewing and recording achievement during their school life. It is also a means of recording subsequent achievement. It is flexible enough to record the achievements of young people of all abilities; those with learning difficulties can use tapes and photos to demonstrate their achievements. This is excellent. But the student has to learn how to use the NRA in preparing a job application, to select from it the documents judged relevant to the interview, and to understand how to use the material to good effect during an interview. The Government-provided folder has a professional quality which will make a good impression if a student has it available for use at an interview. But with any interviewer's time at a premium, it needs to be used skilfully and selectively.

6.7 The NRA has another potential role beyond recording achievement. In a society that needs to be committed to life-long learning, a vital competence that should be mastered during the later stages of statutory education is the management of one's own learning. This includes setting personal objectives, monitoring performance, reviewing work plans in the light of achievement, and reviewing both short-term objectives and long-term aspirations.

6.8 To that end, a separate self-contained section of the NRA (which is not relevant in an interview context) is desirable. This should be supported by the Government through the provision of specifically devised work-sheets.

6.9 The statutory requirement to report on progress using the format of the sheets in the NRA takes effect at the age of 16. But I see great advantage in students who are approaching 14, when they need to be taking decisions about their last two years of statutory schooling, beginning to take responsibility for managing their own learning. In particular, with the help of careers advisers, teachers and employers, they should be thinking through where they want to be at 16 and beyond, and how to achieve this. Real scope for such decision-taking is provided by the planned freeing-up of 40 per cent of schools' curriculum time in Key Stage 4 from September 1996 (and 50 per cent in Wales).

6.10 The beginning of the student-centred action-planning and target-setting processes, signified by presentation of the NRA folder to a student, can be seen as a 'coming of age'. It could be a motivator for disaffected students. When the folder is presented to the student, a separate letter should go to the home, building on the significance of this 'decision-taking step', and attempting to involve parents or carers in the planning and decisions that lie ahead.

6.11 After 16, the use of the NRA is optional except in Government-funded initiatives, and research shows less use after 16. In 1992, only a third of 16–24 year olds were using the NRA and the processes which underpin it. It is, however, directly relevant in the 16–19 phase of personal development. At this stage it has an increasingly important potential role, not only for the purpose of demonstrating achievement to an employer or university admissions tutor, but also in planning learning. Engaging in target-setting and action-planning raises standards of achievement. Improving the effectiveness and extending the use of the NRA in schools and colleges, and beyond that in universities and in employment, could make a valuable contribution to effective learning and in developing and using the skills underpinning life-long learning.

6.12 The DfEE already has work in hand identifying good practice in linking school work on the NRA with the action planning process through careers guidance. Good practice needs to be publicised to schools, colleges and universities. When initial teacher training includes the use of the NRA by trainee teachers for their own development, it increases the effective use of the NRA by those teachers with their students. They also become excellent role models.

6.13 In the further education sector, ten colleges and fourteen sixth-form colleges have been involved in a FEDA development project to embed approaches to recording achievement and action planning in the programmes of all learners. A bulletin issued by FEDA offers guidance on how individual action plans and NRAs can be used to raise achievement and help progression to the next stages of education and training. But keeping up the recording, reviewing and action planning process of the NRA demands effort, even from well-guided young people, teaching staff and employers.

6.14 Though the Confederation of British Industry (CBI) and employers generally have been committed supporters of the NRA, and some three-quarters of large firms use it, consultation during this review tended to confirm research findings that only half of all employers knew of it, and only a quarter use it in some way. If busy employers are to take an interest, they need to see its value and how it can be integrated into the *Investors in People* award and other similar initiatives. The NRA and the processes it seeks to embed must reflect the needs of employers, especially those of small employers.

6.15 In an NRA, employers are looking beyond nationally recognised awards for evidence of qualities and achievements which vary according to the level and kind of job vacancy they are looking to fill. Examples of those which can be reflected in an NRA, without making it bureaucratic, are:

- reliability, in terms of attendance and punctuality (patterns established at school are a good predictor in later life);

- good inter-personal skills, including experience of team working;

- good presentational skills, perhaps demonstrated through interview skills and ability to use an NRA to good effect;

- evidence of breadth of interest as exemplified by work in the community, or participation in initiatives such as the Duke of Edinburgh's Award Scheme, Young Enterprise, youth organisations, sports teams, membership of a choir or drama group;

- competence in a range of skills (and a description of the context in which these skills have been developed and demonstrated).

6.16 The NRA might also recognise evidence of other personal qualities such as reliability, loyalty and leadership.

6.17 These personal qualities that can be recorded in NRAs, not necessarily to be evidenced by documentation at interviews, should be reviewed by students or trainees with the help of the NRA before they make an application and as they prepare for interviews.

6.18 To have value in the eyes of employers and admissions tutors the qualities outlined above need to be well evidenced. Employers and universities will soon reject a system that lacks real substance and rigour. The Government could invite interested groups, perhaps led by the TECs, to get a common understanding of what is valued, and more importantly to help develop the standards required. These agreed standards should be met within existing processes for quality assurance.

6.19 The NRA and the process underlying it could now benefit from the kind of review that any initiative needs from time to time. This should focus on giving it the greatest possible value for the learner or trainee, practicability from the school and college point of view, and standing with university admissions tutors and employers. Such a review would necessarily involve employers, schools, further education, higher education, careers education and guidance professionals and the learners too.

6.20 No other country in Europe has an NRA. We need to be an achievement-orientated society, with all worthwhile achievement encouraged and recognised. All of us need an effective means by which to recognise and communicate to others what it is that we have achieved and what we know, understand and are able to do. The NRA is a well-conceived initiative that responded to the needs of the time, but if it is to fulfil the ambitions of its creators, it now needs review and a relaunch. The review should take account of the current work looking at its format and wider use and of the National Council for Vocational Qualifications (NCVQ's) Individual Portfolio project, which would provide individual jobseekers across the European Community with a common format for presenting information about themselves to potential employers.

6.21 I **recommend** that, with the support of employers:

- The NRA should be reviewed and relaunched, possibly under a new name which would reflect its wider role in personal development.

- The NRA should have a major role in developing skills in planning and managing one's own learning through a self-contained section, based on specially designed worksheets, which guides the student through the process. The section should be worked out in consultation with schools and colleges. (In colleges, the use of 'learning agreements', through which students set targets for their own learning, will support the development of these skills, and contribute directly to the restructured NRA.)

- During 16–19 education and training, consideration should be given to assessing and certificating young people's skills in planning and managing their own learning. This could be done through NCVQ's unit, 'improving own learning and performance'. Although formal assessment of these skills should be optional, recognition of the award of the NCVQ unit should be given in the Universities and Colleges Admissions Service (UCAS) proposed new profile and tariff.

- The NRA should be introduced when decisions are being taken about the last two years of statutory schooling, say at $13^1/_2$ years rather than at 16. The present quality folder provided by the Government should be available to students at that age.

- Use of the NRA throughout life time learning should be strongly encouraged and supported by the Government, employers, LEAs, TECs, schools, colleges, universities and other institutions.

- Use of the NRA as a tool for life time learning should be encouraged through Investors in People.

- All students should receive guidance from schools and colleges on using the NRA in applying for university places and jobs, and in interviews.

■ Consideration should be given to making the NRA processes of recording achievement and action planning part of the schools and colleges inspection frameworks.

■ The existing 'Qualifications and Credits' sheet in the NRA should be entitled the 'Record of National Awards' to record all qualifications and units recognised at national level as part of the national framework outlined in Section 3 of this Report.

SECTION 7

Improving skills for work and lifetime learning

The problem

7.1 The need to improve standards in the skills of communication and the application of number amongst young people was the most frequently expressed concern during the extensive consultation undertaken for this Review. It emerges clearly and strongly from the summary of the views expressed. (See Section 2.)

7.2 In addressing these concerns, it should be acknowledged that they derive in part from the overloading of the first National Curriculum, and from a continual stream of subsequent changes to it which absorbed energies which should have been deployed in teaching. It is also right to recognise the achievements of schools, especially primary schools, in adapting to a curriculum covering ten or more subjects (including science and technology and Welsh in Wales), to children from the age of five. Our children are now getting a broad and balanced education.

7.3 Competence in communication, the application of number and information technology are treated in this Report as key skills for all our young people. Few concerns were expressed about information technology, which schools have successfully integrated into the National Curriculum.

7.4 Many commentators, and employers in particular, have stressed the importance of developing wider skills including inter-personal skills, particularly team-working, presentational skills, a problem-solving approach, and the ability to 'manage one's own learning'. In a society which needs increasingly to be committed to life-long learning, this last is a key to all the rest. A recent survey by The Institute of Directors, for example, showed almost total support for life-long learning.

7.5 The emphasis placed on the key skills during consultation was strong. Concern over standards in communication and the application of number are not new. This does not, however, reduce the need for a response which will improve our performance relative to that of other nations.

7.6 This Section of the Report deals in turn with:

- Historical comparisons.

- Recent responses to the need to raise standards.

- Proposals for developing key skills through the qualifications framework and institutional policies.

- Proposals for promoting personal and interpersonal skills through changes in institutional policy.

46

Historical comparisons

7.7   Employers and universities have regularly expressed concern about inadequate skills among school-leavers.

7.8   For example in 1961, in a public lecture entitled *The Coming Crisis in English,* the then senior Chief Inspector of Schools referred to a decision by the Universities of Oxford and Cambridge to require candidates to take a paper on the use of English. He said:

> 'with the standards of written and spoken English notoriously low at all levels throughout the country, this is a big and salutary and overdue reform.'

7.9   The 1975 Report of the Bullock Committee, *A Language for Life,* says this on its first page:

> 'Many allegations about lower standards today come from employers, who maintain that young people joining them from school cannot write grammatically, are poor spellers, and generally express themselves badly. The employers sometimes draw upon past experience for comparisons, but even where they do not there is a strong implication that at one time levels of performance were superior. It is therefore interesting to find in the Newbolt Report of 1921 observations of a very similar kind. There Messrs. Vickers Ltd reported "great difficulty in obtaining junior clerks who can speak and write English clearly and correctly, especially those aged from 15 to 16 years". Messrs. Lever Bros, Ltd, said: "it is a great surprise and disappointment to us to find that our young employees are so hopelessly deficient in their command of English". Boots Pure Drug Co. remarked "teaching of English in the present day schools produces a very limited command of the English language.... Our candidates do not appreciate the value of shades of meaning, and while able to do imaginative composition, show weakness in work which requires accurate description, or careful arrangement of detail". The last is very close to some of the observations made today, half a century later, and might almost have been taken from evidence submitted to us.'

7.10 In arithmetic, as number was once called, HM Inspector of Schools reported in 1876:

> 'Many who are in a position to criticise the capacity of young people who have passed through the public elementary schools have experienced some uneasiness about the condition of arithmetical knowledge and teaching at the present time. It has been said, for instance, that accuracy in the manipulation of figures does not reach the same standard which was reached twenty years ago. Some employers express surprise and concern at the inability of young persons to perform simple numerical operations involved in business.'

7.11 The Board of Education Report of 1925 included the following passage:

> 'The standard of mathematical ability of entrants to trade courses is often very low..... Experience shows that a large proportion of entrants have forgotten how to deal with simple vulgar and decimal fractions, have very hazy ideas on some easy arithmetical processes, and retain no trace of knowledge of algebra, graphs or geometry, if, in fact, they ever did possess any. Some improvements in this position may be expected as a result of the raising of the school leaving age, but there is as yet no evidence of any marked change.'

7.12 It has been suggested that the replacement of imperial units of measurement by the decimal system, in reducing the need for fractions and other arithmetical calculations, has also reduced the use of mental arithmetic.

7.13 The continuing concern about mathematical and number skills was reflected in the appointment of a Committee of Inquiry into the Teaching of Mathematics in Schools in 1981 (the Cockcroft Committee). Significantly, two particular concerns expressed by the Committee relate to the two competences that concern employers most today:

■ 'We have already referred several times to the need to be able to carry out straightforward calculations mentally' (paragraph 254).

■ 'The earlier chapters of this report make it clear that ability to estimate is important not only in many kinds of employment but in the ordinary activities of adult life' (paragraph 257).

7.14 The Committee found, however, that mental arithmetic occupied a far less prominent position within most mathematics teaching in schools than in former times. This led them to confirm the comments of many of those they had interviewed, that students had been given little or no practice in mental calculation at secondary school, especially after the second year (paragraphs 202 and 254). They found that estimation was not practised in many classrooms (paragraph 258).

7.15 There is ample evidence, therefore, that our present problems are not new. But in arithmetic, the arrival of the calculator has introduced a new factor. The extent of the use of calculators in mathematics is a controversial and still unresolved issue. Calculators have been present in the classroom and examination hall for well over a decade now, and there is still no common accord on their use. They are becoming increasingly complex, and their power is impacting on the curriculum, to the extent that the current emphasis is on improving powers of basic mathematics and reducing the use of calculators. But especially at higher levels, there are real debates to be held on whether it is appropriate to devote substantial amounts of time to teaching techniques that machines can handle much more quickly and efficiently. No-one is asking young people to become human calculators, but they should be able to handle basic arithmetical operations without resort to a calculator; have some facility in mental arithmetic; have a sense of number; be able to estimate; and be able to look at numbers with an understanding of the messages they are giving.

7.16 Whatever may be said, on standards today or in the past, there is a real problem over standards in communication and the application of number. Employers and institutions of higher and further education are seeking a substantial response from schools and colleges.

Recent responses to the need to improve skills in communication and the application of number

7.17 Because the problem of lack of skills in communication and the application of number has been expressed previously and recognised, there have been a number of responses over recent years.

5–16 year olds

7.18 For those between the ages of 5 and 16, the following initiatives have been taken recently or are under consideration.

- The content of the National Curriculum was reduced with effect from September 1995 for 5–14 year olds, and will be reduced for 14–16 year olds in September 1996, in all subjects except mathematics, English and Welsh. This change gave a clear message to schools on the importance of literacy, oracy and numeracy.

- Increased emphasis has been given to number in the curriculum for primary schools, and the standard required for English at level 1 has been markedly increased.

- Increased emphasis is being given to number and algebra in the Key Stage tests, and an increased time allocation is to be given to testing mathematics for 11 year olds in 1996.

- A mathematics test paper which prohibits the use of calculators will be introduced for 11 year olds in 1996. A similar move is under consideration for 14 year olds in 1997, along with the introduction of a short assessment of mental arithmetic within the mathematics tests at both ages.

- For English, consultation has taken place in England on more detailed reporting to parents with separate reporting of achievement in reading, writing and spelling by 11 year olds.

- Consideration is being given to the relationship between the expected standards of attainment in English at age 14, and those expected two years later in the General Certificate of Secondary Education (GCSE) examination, to ensure that there is appropriate progression.

- New criteria have been introduced for primary phase courses of initial teacher training, requiring at least 150 hours' training to teach each of the National Curriculum core subjects. For example, at least 50 hours of the provision for mathematics must be devoted to teaching arithmetic, and at least 50 hours of the provision for English teaching must be devoted to teaching reading.

- A network of literacy and numeracy centres is being developed in England to improve the quality of teaching in primary schools.

16–19 year olds

7.19 For the 16–19 age group with which this Review is concerned, similar initiatives include the following:

- Reserving 5 per cent of the marks in GCSE examinations for spelling, punctuation and grammar.

- A decision at the end of 1995 to resume a previous practice of showing separately the level of achievement in the oral use of language in the GCSE result for English and Welsh.

- The introduction of a 'Quality of Language' requirement into the A level Code of Practice to ensure that candidates' use of language (including clarity of expression, structure and presentation of ideas, spelling, punctuation and grammar) is assessed in the A level examination.

- Introduction by the National Council for Vocational Qualifications (NCVQ) of units in communication, the application of number and information technology, with no award being made at any level of a GNVQ unless the candidate has met the required standards.

- A policy that all those pursuing Modern Apprenticeships are provided with opportunities to achieve the above NCVQ units in addition to National Vocational Qualifications (NVQs).

7.20 These are all necessary developments, and where there are problems in their implementation, they are being addressed. In Wales, improvements in the skills of language and numeracy are at the heart of the distinctive 'Bright Future' programme designed to raise educational standards in all schools there.

Developing the key skills

7.21 The main response to the concerns expressed by employers and further and higher education must unquestionably lie in education before 16. As discussed earlier, revisions to the National Curriculum should support this aim. But we have an immediate problem which requires a response over the next few years for those between 16 and 19. And there are other reasons for giving attention during these years to developing key skills in communication, the application of number and, to a lesser extent, information technology. These include the following:

- There is a gap between the skills required in the workplace and those commonly offered by the new entrants to work.

- There is a need to continue developing these skills in post-16 education; unless used, the skills deteriorate.

- Students benefit from experience of applying the skills in context. A strong message was that skills developed in school mathematics and English or Welsh lessons need development in a range of contexts.

- Information technology is fast developing, and students need opportunities to maintain, develop, and update their skills.

7.22 The following paragraphs look at each of the three existing qualifications pathways. For students between 16 and 19, some development of existing practice is proposed across all three pathways, together with a new AS in the three key skills to secure and promote better standards.

Key skills and GCSEs

7.23 In a policy drive to raise standards in communication and the application of number, and to confirm the growing competence of young people in the use of information technology, it is particularly relevant to consider what incentives to improve performance might be given through the GCSE examination itself. As a recent CBI survey shows, employers attach importance to GCSEs when they recruit young people. A small study carried out with employers on behalf of the Review suggests that the new GCSEs in English and mathematics cover what employers want[1]. The problem lies less with content than with the emphasis given to the various elements in teaching and assessment at GCSE.

7.24 I **recommend** that:

- To underline the importance of number, the regulatory and awarding bodies should provide a separate grading for those aspects of GCSE mathematics concerned with calculation, estimation and statistics. This grade would be shown separately on the face of the certificate. This would complement the recent proposal by the Secretaries of State to give a separate grading for spoken English and Welsh alongside the overall grade for the GCSE in these subjects. Further recommendations which relate to mathematics are made in Section 10.

- In information technology (for which a range of full, combined-subject or short course GCSEs and other vocational qualifications already exists, but none of which is necessarily taken by all students)[2] the NCVQ units in information technology should be approved as a basis for assessment at Key Stage 4 in schools. Schools should be encouraged to offer appropriate information technology qualifications to all pupils.

Key skills and A levels

7.25 The need for the further development of communication skills, in particular oracy, and numeracy among A level students, was stated frequently in the evidence given to the Review. In the research with young people themselves, A level students felt they were less likely than GNVQ students to be armed with certain communication skills (eg giving presentations), team skills (eg working in a group), and computer skills (eg word processing), which they felt would be useful for higher education and employment. The issue is how best to respond. Though there has been little concern expressed by employers about the need to raise standards in the use of information technology, these skills are as necessary to A level students as to those pursuing other qualifications. It will be increasingly important in the coming years that people at all levels can use information technology effectively.

7.26 It has been argued that it would be wrong, especially for students who find their A level programmes demanding, to make the further development of the three key skills mandatory beyond GCSE. With about 30 per cent of those embarking on A level courses not obtaining the two passes frequently required to secure university entrance, this is a telling argument. It could be a significant burden for students, depending on their subject choice and the number of subjects taken, and a particularly heavy burden for mature part-time students. Action is however needed.

---

[1] A workshop for employers hosted by the East Mercia Chamber of Commerce, November 1995. Employers were asked to consider whether they would employ 16–19 year olds with a range of numerical and communication skills based on GCSE grading criteria and level 2 NCVQ application of number and communication units.

[2] There is currently a wide range of courses that include information technology approved under Section 5 of the Education Reform Act, 1988. Seven awarding bodies account for eight full information technology GCSEs, six full GCSEs combined with business and seven information technology short courses. There are also several non-GCSE information technology courses currently available.

7.27 I therefore **recommend** that the A level subject cores and syllabuses should be reviewed by the appropriate regulatory and awarding bodies to identify what further scope there is to build in relevant elements in communication, the application of number and information technology without distorting the integrity of individual subjects.

7.28 This should help to provide opportunities for students to practise these skills in the context of their A level subjects and raise standards. However, the scope for this approach will vary between subjects. A strong and more specific incentive to students and institutions is needed to give a more powerful focus to action to raise standards. This is best achieved through the availability of awards which recognise skills in communication, the application of number and information technology, and which carry a numerical score both in the proposed UCAS new tariff and in performance tables.

7.29 The three key skill units required in GNVQs offer one way of recognising these achievements. However I **recommend** that in addition to this, students should have the opportunity to develop their key skills by taking a new 'AS in key skills'. The level of performance in each of the skills of communication, the application of number, and information technology would be separately recognised in the award, and contribute to the overall grade. A minimum level of achievement in each skill would be required for an award. (See Appendix G5 on a reformulated AS.)

7.30 The proposal for a new AS in key skills is not made as a mandatory requirement for the award of A levels, but to encourage students to recognise that these skills are essential for work and adult life, regardless of the qualifications pathway followed between 16 and 19. I see this new AS as a major element in the proposals from this Review. I **recommend** that the majority of students should be encouraged to seek it; that universities should make clear that they value it; that employers should make it a specific issue in their recruitment; and that it should provide a way of satisfying the mandatory requirements for the new certificate and diploma recommended in Section 8.

7.31 I **recommend** that the joint committee of the NCVQ and SCAA proposed in Section 4 of this Report should review the present requirements for the three key skills in the Advanced level in the GNVQ, with a view to considering the extent to which there should be common standards for the GNVQ and the proposed new AS in key skills. Such work will however need to recognise that the requirement for key skills in the GNVQ specifies a minimum level to support the main areas of study. The new AS will be a separate graded award, which builds on the skills developed pre-16. The development of the proposed AS award provides an excellent opportunity for the regulatory bodies to work together. In the light of policy guidance from these bodies, it would then be for awarding bodies to specify jointly what is required. The essence of the award would lie in the skills being demonstrated in a context broadly relevant to the main areas of knowledge covered by A levels. To provide context, perhaps 40 per cent of the marks might be available from coursework arising from the student's A level work, with the remaining 60 per cent depending upon examination, contextualised so far as possible for the main areas of knowledge.

7.32 This would make the qualification more attractive to students who already develop their key skills through their main A level studies. To minimise the cost of provision, the awarding bodies could be invited to collaborate over the development of syllabuses.

Key skills and GNVQs

7.33 All GNVQs incorporate the NCVQ units in communication, the application of number and information technology as a mandatory requirement. The first concern is to ensure the effective working of present requirements. The Further Education Funding Council (FEFC) in a recent report on GNVQs (November 1995) found cause for concern in the majority of colleges inspected over the development and assessment of these three skills.

7.34 Research into the GNVQ by the Gloucestershire College of Arts and Technology and the University of the West of England (1995), has found that GNVQ students do not develop the skills of note taking and essay writing required in many degree courses. It would be useful to review the content of these units in the light of feedback from higher education and employment.

7.35 I **recommend** that these issues should be taken into account in the work of the NCVQ/SCAA joint committee, together with the views of employers and universities.

7.36 I welcome the work that NCVQ is already taking forward on the external assessment of units in communication, the application of number and information technology. A small project has already surveyed key and other skill units developed by NCVQ to determine what might be assessed externally[3]. There will be further consultations and work to develop appropriate external assessments aimed at improving rigour and making assessment more manageable and cost-effective.

7.37 I further **recommend** that:

- The NCVQ should consider the use of appropriately designed, simple-to-use tests for components of the units in communication, the application of number and information technology. These tests should be varied enough to meet a wide range of interests. Such tests could provide a common element between the NCVQ units and the AS in key skills proposed in Sections 7.29 to 7.32.

- The present GNVQ requirements in communication, the application of number and information technology at level 3 should be reviewed alongside the consideration of the new AS in key skills as proposed in Section 7.31.

Key skills and NVQs

7.38 In the NVQ there is no requirement for candidates to demonstrate competence in communication, the application of number and information technology, except when they are an intrinsic requirement for success in the trade or profession concerned. This issue is discussed further in Section 9 of this Report. These NCVQ units are however a feature of Modern Apprenticeships, and will feature strongly in the proposed National Traineeships. (See Section 5.)

7.39 The Report by Mr Gordon Beaumont on the Review of 100 NVQs and SVQs (see Appendix G2) records that employers are 'broadly content with the core skills currently incorporated into standards although with variation between sectors'. He emphasises that the decision about key skills should be left to employers, and that their decision should be driven by whether key skills are required in the occupation.

---

[3]   *Assessment of The Core Skill Units in GNVQ*, NCVQ, 1995 (unpublished), by John Wilmut, Henry Macintosh, and Robert Wood.

However, because they enable transfer between trades and professions, he proposes that they should be available as stand-alone units for those wishing to attain them where they are not a requirement of the job.

7.40 The argument against compulsion, particularly at the lowest levels, is strongly made. It would be wrong if people were denied the opportunity, as a result of requirements in communication, the application of number and information technology, to gain recognition of achievement in their chosen calling. It could be a powerful disincentive to young people seeking to build up a vocational skill if other skills, not immediately needed for the qualifications being sought, put the qualification beyond their reach. Such a requirement would add to the cost of provision, and this might of itself be an obstacle to the take-up of the NVQ.

7.41 Beyond the lowest rungs of the NVQ ladder, skills in communication and the application of number become an increasingly necessary competence. By the time candidates are approaching NVQ level 3, reaching the supervisory level in work terms, these skills are becoming more relevant, and they should be included. I therefore **recommend** further discussion with the lead bodies for the various sections of industry, the awarding bodies and the NCVQ, to assess the case for their explicit inclusion in the specifications where they are an essential requirement for the job.

Encouraging commitment to key skills

7.42 Recognising the weight attached in the consultation to the key skills, I **recommend** that all schools, colleges, and training bodies that receive public funding to provide education and training for 16–19 year olds (including Youth Training, the new National Traineeships and National Entry level provision, and Modern Apprenticeships) should provide opportunities for all young people to develop these skills and to have them assessed. Wherever practicable, such learning should be related to the kind of experience the young person is likely to have in his or her work.

7.43 I also **recommend** that all young people on programmes funded at public expense should be required to take advantage of the facilities offered for developing the key skills.

7.44 I **recommend** that this commitment to developing key skills should be identified as a priority in the development plans of those institutions and monitored by the appropriate regulatory and inspection bodies.

7.45 Finally, I **recommend** that:

■ All those seeking awards in the proposed National Certificates and Diploma (see Section 8) would need to achieve standards in the three key skills through either the proposed AS in key skills or the NCVQ units in communication, the application of number and information technology at level 3.

■ Universities and employers should be urged to make a particular point of making clear to candidates that acquisition of the new AS in key skills (or the NCVQ equivalent) will bear on their recruitment decisions.

■ Teachers should receive help and guidance through programmes of staff development to enable them to provide opportunities for the further development of key skills within A level courses and to prepare them for teaching the new AS in key skills.

Personal and inter-personal skills

7.46 So far the discussion has been entirely in terms of the desirability of higher achievement in communication, the application of number, and the updating and development of skills in the use of information technology. But employers would in particular wish to see the development of inter-personal skills in team working, presentation skills (including skills of oracy and personal presentation), and wider personal skills such as problem-solving and self-management of learning programmes. The value of these is brought out in the CBI survey (see Appendix A4), and was the subject of frequent comment in consultation.

7.47 These are skills that the approach to learning in the GNVQ is calculated to develop. For example, grading within GNVQs is designed to encourage and recognise students who take the initiative and manage their work effectively. There are also additional units in improving one's own learning and performance and in working with others, which GNVQ students may take in addition to the requirements of their award.

7.48 The A level approach to learning undoubtedly develops skills valued by employers, for example skills in analysis and in the critical evaluation of information, but it has not been specifically designed, as the GNVQ was, to develop some of the skills valued by industry. This raises the question whether any initiative should be taken to encourage the development in A level courses of those personal and inter-personal skills which the Review has shown employers value highly.

7.49 The most productive course is likely to lie in creating opportunities to practise these skills and developing them through assessed coursework requirements. For example, students might be required to tackle projects through team working, thus developing inter-personal skills, as well as practice in oral presentations, problem-solving and managing their learning. NCVQ's units in these areas can also be taken with A levels, GNVQs and NVQs, and attract a numerical score in the proposed new UCAS tariff. Personal and inter-personal skills are also developed through the Award Scheme Development and Accreditation Network (ASDAN)[4] and in the Diploma of Achievement (DoA)[5].

7.50 Effective teaching, learning and assessment of these skills will only succeed, however, if it is a firmly established and published policy of the school or college. For example, an institution would need to make an explicit commitment and provide opportunities for students to develop them.

7.51 Recognition of these achievements could be included within the student's National Record of Achievement (see Section 6). The National Record of Achievement, in the form proposed in that section, provides the basis for recognising achievement in the development of skills in the management of learning. This could lead to students seeking the GNVQ unit award for improving their own learning and performance, as proposed in Section 6.

---

[4] ASDAN began as a local initiative in the South West in 1988. There are now approximately 1,500 schools and colleges involved with some 100,000 students involved in its Youth Awards and Further Education Schemes. ASDAN covers the NCVQ units of communication, the application of number and information technology at all levels.

[5] The DoA was launched nationally in February 1995. Some 600 schools and colleges are currently involved and the number is expected to grow to 1,000 by September 1996.

Encouraging commitment to personal and interpersonal skills

7.52 I recommend that:

- All learners, including A level students, should be given opportunities by institutions to practise making oral presentations to peer groups, to engage in discussion on their presentations, and to tackle projects through group work to develop their experience of team working.

- Learners should be encouraged to record their achievements in these skills in their National Record of Achievement and to gain certification through NCVQ units in 'improving own learning and performance' and 'working with others' post-16.

- Institutions should be encouraged to identify opportunities for developing learners' personal and inter-personal skills in their development plans, and this should be monitored by inspection bodies.

S E C T I O N 8

National Targets, National Certificates and the National Advanced Diploma

8.1 During the Review, a case has been made for a distinctive national award to recognise achievement of specified performance both at 16 and at 18–19.

■ One view, represented by the bodies providing education for 16–19 year olds[1], is that there should be an award related to the **National Targets for Education and Training** which would provide a specific target of achievement for the majority of 16–19 year olds.

■ Another view, advocated for example by the National Commission on Education, is that the structure of 16–19 education and training needs to be changed through introducing a broader range of study, and aligning practice in England, Wales and Northern Ireland more closely with that in many other parts of the Western world. Achievement against prescribed criteria would be recognised through a distinctive award.

8.2 This section of the Report reviews both proposals, and offers a response which would accommodate both.

National Certificates for achievement related to the National Targets

8.3 The National Targets are as follows:

■ By age 19, 85 per cent of young people to achieve five GCSEs at grade C or above, an Intermediate GNVQ or a full NVQ level 2.

■ 75 per cent of young people to achieve level 2 competence in communication, numeracy and information technology by age 19; and 35 per cent to achieve level 3 competence in these skills by age 21.

■ By age 21, 60 per cent of young people to achieve two A levels, an Advanced GNVQ or a full NVQ level 3.

8.4 The National Targets are therefore pitched at two levels, Intermediate and Advanced. The main proposal is that a certificate should be awarded to all of those meeting the National Target requirements at these two levels in both the 'main study' and in the three key skills of communication, the application of number and information technology.

---

[1] The Joint Associations Curriculum Group: representing the Association for Colleges, the Girls' Schools Association, the Headmasters' & Headmistresses' Conference, the Secondary Heads' Association, the Sixth Form Colleges' Association, the Society of Headmasters and Headmistresses in Independent Schools and the National Association of Head Teachers.

8.5 Current performance against the National Targets is as follows.

Table 2

	1995 %	Targets for 2000 %	Increase needed (%)
Percentage with 5 GCSEs at grade C or above, an Intermediate GNVQ or full NVQ level 2 by age 19	63	85	22
Percentage with 2 A levels, an Advanced GNVQ or full NVQ level 3 by age 21	44	60	16

8.6 There is still a long way to go to achieve the National Targets. Each year the challenge becomes greater, because it means lifting the performance of those whose achievement needs greatest improvement.

8.7 If the National Targets are to be met, and if achievement in communication, the application of number and information technology is to be raised distinctly above present levels, they need to be the centre of national attention and concern. It means that the targets must be owned by those who are in a position, at all levels, to influence their achievement. LEAs, TECs, and other relevant partners are involved in setting local targets through Strategic Forums. TECs are contractually obliged to report annually to the DfEE on progress against these targets, and the DfEE is currently developing a synthesis of this information. The Government has also recognised the role of Industry Training Organisations (ITOs) in setting targets for industry sectors.

8.8 However, there is a concern about the lack of consistency on how 'baseline' information is calculated, how targets are set and how progress is measured. There is also variation in the extent of the involvement of individual schools and colleges in the process of local target-setting. There should be an effective chain from national to local level for the achievement of these targets, with every secondary school and college aiming to make a contribution to the national goal and action should be taken to that effect.

8.9 To put the targets in clearer focus at the level of the individual school or college, and to give a direct means of measuring achievement against them, it would be possible to introduce National Certificates recognising achievement equal to, or greater than, specified levels. There would therefore be a National Certificate to recognise the target level of achievement at the Intermediate level in the framework of qualifications proposed in the Report, and a National Certificate to recognise achievement at the Advanced level. The underlying authority for the National Certificates would be the certificates issued by the National Awarding Bodies. The National Certificates would recognise achievement built up over time, and combinations of achievement across the three pathways that comply with the national standards. For those in work, the National Certificate might most appropriately be awarded by the TECs, based on inspection of certificates issued by the awarding bodies. For those in full-time education, it would be issued by the school or college.

8.10 The National Targets cover both the level of achievement required in the 'main pathway' and also required levels of competence in communication, the application of number and information technology. The National Certificate proposal brings these two targets together. It would be awarded only to candidates meeting the requirement in the main pathway and in the three key skills. The requirements for the skills in communication, the application of number and information technology would be as follows:

- **At the Advanced Level,** achievement of the NCVQ units in communication, the application of number and information technology at level 3, or the new AS in key skills (see Section 7.29-7.32), these being harmonised to be of the same standard.

- **At Intermediate Level,** achievement of the NCVQ units in communication, the application of number and information technology at level 2, or a GCSE grade C or above in English/Welsh, mathematics and information technology (the latter as a full, combined-subject or short course GCSE).

8.11 By tying the award of the proposed National Certificate both to the required achievement in the main pathway and to the stipulated standard in the three key skills, the proposal made here is putting proportionally more emphasis on achievement of these skills than is done in the National Targets. The argument for so doing is that in a society committed to life-long learning, a pre-condition of success is a good level of competence in the key skills. They are the gateways to learning.

8.12 As noted elsewhere in this Report, employers place much emphasis on personal and inter-personal skills as reflected in team-working, management by students of their own learning, and problem-solving. These are a feature of the GNVQ and to some extent of the NVQ. For A level students, it is recommended in Section 7.46-7.52 that schools and colleges should build into their teaching programmes opportunities for students to have experience of team and project working in which they engage in problem-solving, and also opportunities to make presentations to develop their communication skills. The National Targets do not make explicit reference to such skills, but in view of the importance employers attach to these other core skills, they have been taken into account in the recommendations in this Report. Section 6 responds to the concern to develop skills in the management of one's own learning.

Recognising achievement beyond the threshold

8.13 The proposals outlined above would be the minimum requirements for the National Certificate at each level. The National Certificate would also record all achievement above the prescribed minimum.

8.14 In consultation, the importance of promoting and recording achievement beyond the threshold of the National Certificate was often emphasised, particularly at the Advanced level. Additional units and awards achieved should be recorded on the certificate. For purposes of entry to higher education, UCAS is currently developing a new profile and qualifications tariff to provide information to admissions tutors that will include all of a candidate's achievements. (See Appendix F3.)

8.15 I **recommend** that a National Certificate should be introduced to recognise achievement at the Intermediate and Advanced levels. The requirements for each level should be as follows:

- **Intermediate level:** a minimum of 5 GCSEs at grade C or above, including English or Welsh, mathematics, and the full, combined-subject or short course

GCSE in information technology[2]; or a GNVQ at Intermediate level; or a full NVQ at level 2. Where GCSEs in English or Welsh, mathematics and information technology have not been achieved at grade C or above, competence must be demonstrated in the NCVQ units of communication, the application of number and information technology at level 2.

- **Advanced level:** two A level passes, or a full GNVQ at the Advanced level, or a full NVQ at level 3, plus competence in communication, the application of number and information technology demonstrated through the NCVQ units at level 3, or through the new AS in the three key skills, these being harmonised to be of the same standard.

- Consideration should be given to the creation of a National Certificate at the Foundation level. This would require at least five GCSEs at grades D to G (including English or Welsh, mathematics and an appropriate qualification in information technology); or a full GNVQ at Foundation level; or a full NVQ level 1. Where GCSEs in English or Welsh, mathematics and information technology have not been achieved, competence must be demonstrated in the NCVQ units of communication, the application of number and information technology at level 1.

- Work should be carried out to identify those other major awards which should count for recognition towards the achievement of the National Certificate at the Intermediate and Advanced levels.

- The National Certificates should be designed to recognise achievement over and above the minimum requirements for the award.

- The Government should work with LEAs, TECs and other relevant partners to ensure that the setting, monitoring and achievement of local targets is consistent with, and contributes to, the National Targets for Education and Training.

- In addition LEAs, TECs, and the Further Education Funding Councils should work with locally managed and grant maintained schools and colleges on setting, monitoring and achieving institutional targets linked to the National Certificates.

- The Government should consider the case for governing bodies of schools and colleges reporting on progress against institutional targets as part of the annual report to parents and the wider community.

- The National Certificates should be issued by schools and colleges and for those at work, by TECs, on the basis of awards made by the awarding bodies, with strong arrangements to ensure tight control over the granting of certificates and safeguards against fraudulent practice.

A National Diploma at the Advanced level to encourage studies in depth, with complementary studies to give breadth

8.16 The first proposal addresses the need to achieve the National Targets for Education and Training for the year 2000, and to raise standards in communication, the application of number and information technology. But it does not address the need to encourage greater breadth of studies in terms of different subjects and qualifications

---

2 Due allowance could be made for particular requirements in Wales, such as the possible inclusion of science.

at 16 plus. During research (see Appendix B4) the A level students in the discussion groups had, on reflection, regretted having to make early choices which would be likely to determine their future plans. In some cases they had found their choice of course at university had been restricted because of the A levels they had studied. Others had found it difficult grappling with new subjects which had not been studied at A level. As a result some students (17 per cent in the case of A level students) indicated they would have preferred to study a broader range of subjects. The issue of how to introduce greater breadth at this level has been the subject of much discussion during consultation, and indeed has been debated for many decades.

8.17 It is now forty years since the government of the day appointed the Crowther Committee to advise on education for 15–18 year olds. The Committee was asked in particular to consider the balance between specialisation and breadth of study. The issue has been debated ever since, although today it is not only a debate about a balanced range of studies or subject breadth, but also about how far it would be desirable to encourage students to consider combining academic with vocational studies.

8.18 The Crowther Committee recognised the singularity of current practice in the sixth form in England of selecting two or three subjects for serious study. The Committee said: 'Neither in Western Europe nor in North America is there anything of the sort. Even nearer to home in Scotland the schools insist on a much wider spread of subjects in the sixth form than we do in England.' (Paragraph 379.)

8.19 Nevertheless, after reviewing the arguments (Chapter 25), the Committee concluded that in-depth study of two or three subjects was desirable. The Committee argued that this approach recognised the readiness and eagerness of young people at the age of 16 to engage in serious study of a subject or subjects which reflected their preferences and enthusiasms. They saw it as developing a degree of mastery of the subject that led students to go exploring beyond the text books and to begin to assume responsibility for their own learning. They considered that by the end of the sixth form, with the right teaching, students would begin to see how their chosen areas of study fitted together, and to be curious about how these fitted into the whole field of knowledge. The Committee saw this approach as teaching students to think.

8.20 The Crowther Committee went on to argue, however, that the remaining quarter, or third, of sixth form time needed to be put to better use than was then the case. They argued that it should be used for two distinctive purposes:

■ Activities shared by arts and science students together (religious education and all that goes into the formation of moral standards; art and music; and physical education).

■ Literacy for science specialists and numeracy for arts specialists (with literacy being taken as skills in the use of the mother tongue and the development of moral, aesthetic and social judgement; and numeracy meaning not only the ability to reason quantitatively but also some understanding of scientific method and some acquaintance with scientific achievements).

8.21 This was therefore an argument for depth of study, complemented by use of the remaining time to give some breadth.

8.22 In reaching those conclusions, the Crowther Committee made it explicit that they were based on what they considered to be educationally valid principles, rather than on what was needed to meet the entry requirements of universities. However, in considering what might motivate schools and pupils to take this approach seriously, the Committee concluded that the most potent influence was likely to be the knowledge that prospective employers, universities and colleges attached importance to them.

8.23 The Robbins Report on Higher Education followed a few years later. This made it clear that the intensity of competition for university places was powerful in determining the school curriculum and the associated specialisation. To quote from the Report:

> 'There has developed a strong tendency to concentrate on preparation for the Advanced level examination and on the subjects most closely relevant to securing entry into higher education and into the universities in particular. This has led to a reduction, sometimes very drastic, in the time devoted to other subjects and, within the subjects that are being studied for examination, to a range of work often much narrower than would have been chosen in less competitive circumstances.' (Chapter 7, paragraph 202).

8.24 The Robbins Committee also noted complaints from some institutions of higher education that some students could not express themselves clearly in English, and had an inadequate understanding of elementary mathematical principles.

8.25 The Crowther proposals to bring breadth into the sixth form curriculum seem to have yielded to the effects of competition for university places. The pressure which the Committee sought from employers and higher education, to support the wider studies they had recommended in English and numeracy, did not materialise.

8.26 It was in this context that the first A level in General Studies was introduced in 1959 to give a focus and identity to non-specialist studies in the sixth form. It was followed by a series of initiatives designed to promote non-specialist studies. These included an *Agreement to Broaden the Curriculum* in 1961, whereby 360 secondary schools committed themselves to devote a third of sixth form time to non-A level studies. Reports by the Secondary Schools Examination Council in 1960 and 1962 also warned of the dangers of over-specialisation. General Studies is now a widely-used means of broadening the curriculum, and is the second most popular A level in terms of entries. Its role in the context of breadth of study post-16 is considered in Section 12.

8.27 In 1969, the Schools Council and the Standing Conference on University Entrance made a joint statement that there were reasons for dissatisfaction with the sixth form curriculum. It was too narrow, it forced pupils to make premature choices, and it failed to take account of the widening range of ability in the sixth forms as they grew in size. Various proposals were made to respond to this dissatisfaction, including the so-called Q (qualifying exam) in five subjects after one year's study, with the F (further level) in three subjects in the second year.

8.28 Further working parties of the Schools Council, established in the 1970s, proposed a two level syllabus and examination structure with N (normal) and F (further) levels. The norm for students would have been five examination subjects, of which not more than two would have been studied to F level. The N and F were to replace A levels. An immense amount of work followed as the decade progressed, through sixteen syllabus steering groups, to develop these proposals in detail. Studies in schools showed that they were able to design a five subject curriculum based on the N and F levels. At the end of the decade these proposals were abandoned in favour of retaining A levels.

8.29 The Higginson Committee in 1988, with much support from the universities, returned to the case for breadth. It proposed that the typical three A levels should be replaced by five leaner A levels, the necessary space being provided by drawing upon the time identified by the Crowther Committee. This approach was not acceptable to the Government because of concerns about diluting the standards of A levels.

8.30 The difference between practice in England, Wales and Northern Ireland, and practice elsewhere in the developed world, remains. Meanwhile participation in post-16 education and entry into higher education have expanded greatly. The comparison between 1955 and 1994–95 in England is telling.

Table 3

Participation Rates	1955 %	1994–95 (%)
Percentage continuing in full-time education at 17	10	59
Percentage of 18–19 year olds proceeding into higher education	4	31

8.31 Given this expansion, it should at least be for consideration whether the arguments that led the Crowther Committee to its conclusion, which were based on the needs of 10 per cent of the cohort, are equally valid for the 59 per cent continuing in full-time education today, and more specifically for the third who attempt A levels. A further reason for re-examining that Committee's conclusions lies in today's realisation that in the next century the need to change direction in careers will certainly be greater, possibly much greater, than in the present century.

8.32 This strengthens the case for an option for those young people who do not see themselves as potential subject specialists in their careers, and are seeking a form of post-16 education which provides the educational benefit that comes from a study in depth, but complemented by studies in other areas. This combination would provide a basis for a range of careers. The need for an option combining depth of study in one or two areas, with complementary breadth in others, is also relevant to the range of provision in higher education in the next century.

8.33 Currently an opportunity to pursue a broad course of studies post-16 is provided through the International Baccalaureate. This has been available internationally for 30 years. But it has been taken up by only a small minority of schools and colleges. Representatives of the International Baccalaureate Organisation indicated in discussions that even though students follow a demanding programme, they have some ground to make up when they progress to university in the subjects chosen for the degree programme.

8.34 This is not to say that schools and colleges have been uninterested in breadth. Many have offered excellent opportunities for students to develop beyond conventional academic pursuits. But breadth, in the form adopted in much of the developed world, has not characterised education in the United Kingdom, outside Scotland.

8.35 The Government has, however, undertaken a number of initiatives to encourage a broader range of studies. The Government's 1991 White Paper on *Education and Training for the Twenty-First Century* noted that 'the specialised study of two or three subjects, often closely related to each other, is for many students too narrow a preparation for the next stage of study or work.' Options should be sufficiently wide to meet the needs of students wanting to combine breadth with depth.

8.36 The Advanced Supplementary (AS), equivalent in weight to half an A level, was introduced in 1987 to encourage greater breadth, but take-up has remained disappointingly small: in 1995 only one AS was taken for every 15 A levels. The reasons include doubts about its currency with university admissions tutors, difficulty in accommodating it within the timetable, and the commonly-held view that the study of two ASs as currently constituted is more demanding than the study of a single A level.

8.37 Concern about our national practice has remained. As noted in the Interim Report, there have been several proposals for greater breadth of study, most notably by the National Commission on Education. They recommended a General Education Diploma at two levels, to recognise the successful completion of learning at the typical ages of 16 and 18. The Diploma would recognise achievement in the GCSE, A levels, GNVQ and NVQs.

8.38 This is their proposal in summary.

Table 4

General Education Diploma Ordinary Level	General Education Diploma Advanced Level
Incorporates the requirements of the National Curriculum	In-depth study of a major programme area. (Examples would be: Engineering; Physics and Chemistry; Business Studies and Economics; History; Modern Languages; Art and Design; Environmental Studies)
Prescribed core subjects form roughly half the programme: Use of English; Mathematics; Natural Science; Technology, including information technology; Citizenship; a Modern Foreign Language	Balancing studies in three other programme areas forming between a third and a half of the total programme
A choice of subjects from a wide range of other areas, including the expressive arts and humanities, to provide balance	Core skills

8.39 The National Commission envisaged that these proposals would be the standard for all. But since the whole system of post-16 education in England, Wales and Northern Ireland through to the university degree has been so much based on high achievement between 16 and 19 in a narrow range of subjects, it is extremely difficult to effect change. To adopt breadth at the cost of a four year university degree course in many subjects would raise major issues of funding. Moreover students vary in their interests, and a standard approach would not reflect the range of the student body.

8.40 The proposal in this Report for a programme which combines depth of study with complementary work to give breadth has two key features which distinguish it from the proposal discussed above. First, it is put forward as an option, rather than as a standard requirement for education for all. This avoids the disadvantage of requiring uniformity of approach where there is diversity of talent, aptitudes and enthusiasms amongst students. Second, though breadth is its distinguishing characteristic, it must include two full A levels, or the equivalents in the applied and vocational pathways, to satisfy the normal university entry requirements for depth.

8.41 There should be a distinctive award at the Advanced level as an option to provide for breadth.

8.42 It would share with the proposed target-linked National Certificate the following characteristics:

- A grouped certificate to recognise a prescribed level of achievement, typically at 18 or 19, but available independent of age, and allowing for achievement to be built up over a specified period of time.

- A strong emphasis, as a mandatory requirement, on achievement in the key skills of communication, the application of number and information technology.

- The ability to build up a portfolio of qualifications based on coherent grouping of units and modules.

- Equal acceptability of achievement at the relevant level in the A level, GNVQ and NVQ pathways, and combinations of these.

8.43 To gain this award, a student would need to achieve the elements set out below.

Depth of study requirement

8.44 To ensure that their studies provide the intellectual stimulation which results from detailed exploration of one or two areas in depth, students should be required to gain two A levels or the full GNVQ at the Advanced level[2]. A threshold grade of achievement might be required for this award. This depth requirement would also be satisfied by the achievement of a full NVQ level 3, as in the National Targets for Education and Training.

The three key skills

8.45 A further requirement should be the achievement of competence in communication, the application of number and information technology. These skills would need to be achieved to the same level as specified for the National Certificate at Advanced level, such as through the proposed new AS in key skills, or the corresponding NCVQ units at level 3, these being harmonised to be of the same standard.

---

[2] Section 9 proposes a new 6 unit award, or 'Applied A level' based on the full 12 unit Advanced GNVQ. If this proposal is accepted the two A levels could both be academic or applied A levels, or one of each.

Complementary studies: The A level pathway

8.46 Breadth should be provided by studies in other complementary areas so that, between the studies in depth and those in breadth, four broadly defined areas of study would be covered. For those pursuing the A level pathway, these might be defined as:

- The sciences, technology, engineering, mathematics.

- The arts and humanities (including English and Welsh).

- Modern languages (including Welsh for students for whom it is not their first language).

- The way the community works (including business, economics, government and politics, law, psychology, and sociology).

8.47 To ensure a sufficient level of achievement in each area of study, each should be studied to the minimum of the reformulated AS proposed in Section 11.

8.48 The total number of complementary units required to achieve this award will therefore depend upon whether the main studies in depth are in more than one area of study. Thus, this award could be achieved with two AS awards (6 units) or three AS awards (9 units) in areas complementary to the study in depth, together with the three key skills. In total therefore the distinctive diploma would be achieved for a total of 21 or 24 units. Of these, 12 would be achieved through studies in depth of A levels, 3 for key skills, and 6 or 9 units in complementary areas.

8.49 It is fundamental to the concept of this award that it should require competence in the use of a modern language as defined above. The emphasis here will be on functional competence, particularly in the skills of speaking, listening and reading. The requirement could be met through a reformulated AS, or by three units at level 3 of the National Language Standards (NLS) designed by the Languages Lead Body, and available as NVQ units. Vocational language units are currently being developed by the regulatory bodies at Foundation and Intermediate levels as an alternative to the GCSE short course in a modern foreign language for 14–16 year olds. These should aid progression to post-16 study of the level 3 NLS units.

8.50 Typically, in the academic pathway, the programme could be delivered as three or four subjects in the first year, with concentration on two or three in the second year. Illustrations in Appendix F2 (student A) indicate the sort of combinations which might lead to this award.

Complementary studies: The GNVQ pathway

8.51 For those pursuing the GNVQ pathway, the basic building block should be the GNVQ at Advanced level, plus the three key skills. Because of the breadth of some GNVQs, a single GNVQ might well be sufficient to cover two of the four areas of study suggested in Section 8.46.

8.52 To enable these learners to achieve this award, consideration will need to be given to assigning GNVQs to the four areas of study. This would enable learners choosing to major in this pathway to achieve the award, with the same kind of requirements for complementary studies as learners majoring in the academic pathway. The requirement for achievement in a modern language could be met as set out in Section 8.49. Students B and C in Appendix F2 illustrate possible combinations involving GNVQs.

Complementary studies: The NVQ pathway

8.53 The basic building block would be a full NVQ at level 3. The approach to this Diploma is entirely consistent with Modern Apprenticeship frameworks, and the flexibilities within those frameworks would allow for the award of the National Advanced Diploma to apprentices pursuing the appropriate combination of qualifications.

8.54 As with the other pathways, a modern language would be a mandatory element in the Diploma, at the same standard as for students taking A levels or the GNVQ as their main study.

8.55 Competence in communication, the application of number and information technology would be demonstrated through the NCVQ units at level 3, or through the proposed new AS level in key skills. This again would be mandatory.

8.56 Beyond that, candidates would need to offer units broadly equivalent to 6 GNVQ units designed to give breadth in a vocational context in areas outside the main NVQ. With a range of over 800 NVQs, there is more than enough scope. Alternatively candidates could select GNVQ or A level units from complementary areas. Student D in Appendix F2 illustrates possible combinations involving an NVQ.,

8.57 It is generally acknowledged that NVQs vary considerably in their overall size, and in the size and numbers of their constituent units. If NVQs are to contribute fully to this new award as described above, work will need to be undertaken to establish their size relative to A levels and GNVQs.

Achieving the award

8.58 Providing the basic principles of the award are met, combining elements from the three main pathways should be encouraged because of the complementary approach to learning they offer. The tables in Appendix F2 (students B and C) illustrate the ways in which awards from the A level or GNVQ pathways might be combined.

8.59 An essential feature of the Diploma is that it does not involve the stark alternative outcomes of success or failure. Learners will achieve the individual qualifications, even if they do not achieve sufficient depth or breadth for the Diploma. Another feature is that the Diploma would be achievable over time. This will ensure that it does not exclude part-time learners and those whose participation is intermittent. It is essential that the Diploma helps to motivate learners to continue and return to study, and to aim high.

Names

8.60 Names matter: they need to be easily remembered.

8.61 For the first Certificates canvassed in this section, the proposed titles are:

'The National Advanced Certificate'
'The National Intermediate Certificate'.

8.62 For the award to recognise breadth, the full title should be:

'The National Advanced Diploma'
(perhaps to be known familiarly as 'The Diploma').

The detail

8.63 Further details of the National Advanced Diploma are given in Appendix FI.

8.64 I recommend that:

- A distinctive diploma at Advanced level should be created to recognise achievement in studies both in depth and in breadth to be known as the National Advanced Diploma ('The Diploma').

- The heart of this award would be two full A levels, *or* a full Advanced GNVQ, *or* a full NVQ at level 3, *or* agreed equivalents.

- Breadth would be provided by studies in complementary areas so that between the studies in depth and those in breadth, four broadly defined areas of study would be covered to the minimum of the new AS proposed in Section 11. For A level students, these areas might be defined as:

  - science, technology, engineering and mathematics;

  - modern languages (including Welsh for students for whom it is not their first language);

  - the arts and humanities (including English and Welsh); and

  - the way the community works (including business, economics, government and politics, law, psychology and sociology).

- For the GNVQ and NVQ a complementary approach would be needed, based on coherent groupings of units from subject areas other than the main study, which would include a modern language.

- Studies in supporting areas would need to be at least an AS qualification, or the equivalent, in terms of units from the GNVQ or NVQ.

- In addition, all those seeking this Diploma would need to achieve standards in the three key skills through either the proposed AS in key skills or the NCVQ units in communication, the application of number and information technology at level 3, these being harmonised to be of the same standard.

- The National Advanced Diploma should be issued by schools and colleges on the basis of certificates issued by the National Awarding Bodies, personally signed by the head of the institution. When that is not possible, they should be awarded by any body authorised to award A levels or GNVQs, on the basis of certificates, and on a payment of a fee to cover administration costs.

- For candidates proceeding through the NVQ pathway, the National Advanced Diploma would be issued by TECs, or by any of the authorised awarding bodies on payment of a fee, following confirmation of the underpinning certificates.

SECTION 9

General National Vocational Qualifications, National Vocational Qualifications and other vocational qualifications

The General National Vocational Qualification (GNVQ)

The GNVQ: structure, name and take-up

9.1 It is fundamental to this Review that the GNVQ should retain its present purposes, distinctive characteristics and size. But there are issues relating to structure and name that merit consideration.

9.2 GNVQs were designed as grouped awards, designed to be broadly equivalent in weight at the Foundation and Intermediate levels to four GCSEs[1], and at the Advanced level to two A levels. The size of the full award creates some problems.

9.3 A large grouped award like the GNVQ increases the risk of non-completion. For the student, the fall-back position of the award of single units is valuable. But by themselves, units are a currency with small purchasing power. The available statistics suggest that a substantial number of candidates achieve unit credits rather than a full GNVQ. The following table of outcomes by October 1995 illustrates the problem.

Table 5 October 1995 outcomes for candidates who started in 1993

	1993 Registrations	1995 Unit Certificates	1995 Full GNVQ
Advanced	29,000	8,500 (29%)	13,500 (47%)
Intermediate	36,000	7,000 (19%)	21,000 (58%)
Foundation	5,000	1,000 (20%)	1,000 (20%)

9.4 In the context of broadening the range of options available to students, the size of the GNVQ presents another problem. For example, at the Advanced level, although the student can broaden his or her studies through the range of optional units that is available, the size of the GNVQ effectively commits most students to that pathway. It is true that a proportion takes a supplementary A level, but the demand of the main GNVQ work has meant that achievement so far in the A level has been modest.

9.5 Looking at this issue from the point of view of the student who is primarily attracted by the A level pathway, two A levels plus a full GNVQ at the Advanced level makes a programme whose total weight is equivalent to four A levels. This effectively rules out this option for the majority of young people.

---

[1] For National Target purposes the Intermediate GNVQ equates to five GCSEs.

9.6 These features together may well contribute to substantial numbers of candidates not achieving a full graded GNVQ within two years, and the polarisation between the A level and GNVQ pathways. The potential value for some people of combining elements of both is not realised.

9.7 Happily the Advanced GNVQ is designed in twelve units which (as noted above) are, in aggregate, equal in weight to two A levels. This gives scope for building up achievement in the GNVQ through groupings of six units equal in weight to an A level. If these groups of six units were graded and given a distinctive title, students deciding what they wish to study post-16 would have more options, and students not completing the full course would have something more to show for their efforts than a range of unit credits. Similarly, for the part-time mature student, there could be advantages in substantial recognition of achievement along the way, or when completion of the full course proves impossible. Such an approach would also give the opportunity to bring greater coherence into the framework of qualifications as a whole.

9.8 The coherence of the whole structure of qualifications, and the scope for combining qualifications, would be further enhanced if at the Advanced level of the GNVQ there were to be a grouping of three of its twelve main units to provide a graded qualification equal in size to the AS qualification in the academic pathway.

9.9 Proposals for the grouping of units in an Advanced GNVQ need to recognise and respond to the distinctive structure of the GNVQ. These include the requirement that to gain the award, the student has to reach a specified standard in three units covering the key skills of communication, the application of number and information technology.

9.10 It would accord with the inherent nature of the GNVQ for any award less than the full qualification to meet the specified standards in the three key skill units. Particular consideration would however need to be given to the question whether a three unit award is so far distant from the spirit of a grouped award, as to outweigh the advantages that come from the additional range of choice for the students and the opportunity for recognising substantial achievement that it offers.

9.11 At the lower levels of the GNVQ, the first steps towards the creation of a graded award equal in size to half the full GNVQ (the Part One GNVQ) have already been taken. It is being piloted in England in some 115 schools in 3 subject areas, in 27 schools in Wales and in 9 schools in Northern Ireland. It is to be extended in September of this year to a larger number of institutions, with coverage of six subjects. This Part One GNVQ at the Foundation and Intermediate levels, as it is called, is a self-standing qualification which meets the needs of 14–16 year olds, and can be accommodated alongside the statutory National Curriculum. But it could equally well be adopted for use by 16–19 year olds, and subject to experience with the pilots, I **recommend** it should be.

9.12 Nomenclature is of the second order of importance, but it is nevertheless significant.

9.13 The GNVQ draws its name by derivation from the NVQ. But it is a name difficult to remember in its own right, and the interplay of NVQ, GNVQ and NCVQ tends to get all but the expert confused. Moreover while the NVQ, with over 100 bodies from industry and commerce behind it, and the A levels with 45 years in the market place behind them, have obvious advantages in achieving recognition, the GNVQ has no such advantages. While teachers and students are becoming increasingly aware of the GNVQ, in national terms it is little known. It is evident that a new qualification takes many years to achieve general recognition.

9.14 The Government has therefore proposed in the past that Advanced GNVQs should be retitled 'Vocational A levels'. That has the advantages both of retaining the link with the vocational side and of identifying the programme with the well-established A levels. The one drawback of that name is confusion with the use of the term 'vocational' to describe NVQs. The name 'Vocational A level' has not been taken up since it was proposed. An alternative name was therefore offered for consideration in the Interim Report, the 'Applied A level'. In its evidence to the Review, the National Council for Industry Training Organisations (NCITO) has urged the adoption of the name 'Applied A levels' so that the term 'vocational' can be reserved for qualifications designed to be achieved in the work place. Indications from consultation conferences suggest that the term 'Applied A levels' would be widely welcomed, but not by all. Staff who teach the GNVQ rightly take pride in the achievements of their students. But outside the schools and colleges the name is little known, and it is important that parents, employers and students making their choices of post-16 pathways have a ready understanding of the nature of what is being offered and achieved. The name, Applied A level, has the advantage of bringing home to everyone that the qualification matches A level as a distinctive approach to learning, based on the application of knowledge. To many the thought of studying something that is related to practical applications but is part of the A level family will be attractive. It would help to give parents a better understanding of the value society places on the GNVQ.

9.15 If such a change were to be made at the Advanced level, consideration would have to be given to whether any change should be made at the Foundation and Intermediate levels. Such a decision might be deferred pending the outcomes of consultation on the desirability and focus of a GNVQ above the Advanced level. But one possibility, linking directly into the proposed framework for National Qualifications (see Section 3), would be Applied Intermediate and Applied Foundation levels.

9.16 In summary, I **recommend** that:

- The title 'Applied A level' should replace the GNVQ (Advanced level), and this term should be adopted on all awarding certificates.

- Because of the size of the full GNVQ and the desirability of building up a common structure with A level, the GNVQ should be structured and named as follows:

Full GNVQ of 12 units, plus the three NCVQ units in communication, the application of number and information technology	Applied A level (Double Award)
Six units plus the three NCVQ units in communication, the application of number and information technology.	Applied A level

■ Detailed consideration should also be given to the creation of a three unit award to be known as the Applied AS, to match the AS in the A level family. In that, the GNVQ family would be completed by:

Three prescribed mandatory units   Applied AS

■ Further consultation should be undertaken to establish whether the GNVQs at Intermediate and Foundation levels, and Part One GNVQs, should be renamed. Proposals for consultation could include the names 'Applied Intermediate levels' and 'Applied Foundation levels'.

9.17 Postponing for the moment a discussion on the rigour of the GNVQ and the NVQ, and on the relationship between GNVQs and NVQs dealt with later in this Section, the most effective take-up of the GNVQ and higher-quality outcomes would be achieved by a number of other measures. I **recommend** that:

■ In the Part One GNVQ, and more widely where it would help, the required knowledge and understanding should be stated in the specifications for GNVQs or in the guidance to teachers.

■ In the expansion of the GNVQ into new institutions, and as new subjects are introduced into institutions, the NCVQ and the awarding bodies should maintain rigorous policies to ensure that there is the necessary expertise and equipment.

■ Guidance to students on GNVQ choices should avoid gender stereotyping and be based on individual considerations of suitability, the scope for progression and prospects.

■ In subjects like manufacturing and engineering, where equipment is costly, the Government should be alert to the possibility that take-up could be unreasonably constrained across the country, with the consequence that student and institutional choice is concentrated too heavily on the comparatively low-cost service sectors.

■ Collaboration between institutions, particularly schools and colleges, should be encouraged to ensure that students can be offered a good range of GNVQ options, bearing in mind the need to ensure that the more capital-intensive subjects are covered.

■ The manufacturing and engineering sectors of industry should give strong support to institutions in developing programmes in these areas.

9.18 In relation to the GNVQ, elsewhere in this Report, I also **recommend** that:

■ The three key skill units of the GNVQ at Advanced level in communication, the application of number, and information technology, be harmonised with the content of the proposed AS in key skills in the A level family of qualifications. (See Section 7.29-7.32.)

■ Further work should be undertaken to identify elements common to the A level and the GNVQ at the Advanced level, where programmes in the two pathways cover similar areas of content. (See Section 3.29-3.37.)

■ Closer association of the A level and GNVQ awarding bodies across the present binary line should be encouraged with a view to pooling of expertise in assessment and awarding, and avoiding a proliferation of competing awards. (See Section 4.)

■ Take-up of the GNVQ and NVQ by young people for whom these pathways are particularly suitable should be encouraged through disinterested expert advice to all young people at school. (See Section 14.)

9.19 Business and industry representatives have expressed concern that the GNVQ is not adequately underpinning the NVQ. With only 15 GNVQs planned, and 800 NVQs in existence, there is an obvious problem. The NCVQ has already responded with additional and optional units, but these need to be greatly increased. The NCVQ should be able to look with confidence to the lead bodies that develop NVQ standards to provide the basis for them. The development of these additional GNVQ units will provide a valuable bridge to NVQs and a means of specifying the knowledge and understanding underpinning NVQs. I **recommend** that:

■ Additional units should be developed to extend the choice of units available to GNVQ students, so that they can direct their studies more closely to particular NVQs and build up the required knowledge and understanding underpinning them.

9.20 Sir Michael Heron and I are agreed that there should be close and continuing monitoring of the experience of universities, and of students who have gained places on the basis of the GNVQ to assist the NCVQ in its continuing development of this programme, which is still very new. I so **recommend**.

9.21 At the Entry level to the National Framework of Qualifications (see Section 12) there is a need for young people who are motivated in that direction to have access to applied learning which can receive recognition as proposed in this Report. I **recommend** that:

■ The regulatory and awarding bodies should develop units and qualifications which provide opportunities for applied learning at the proposed Entry level and progression to Foundation level.

The NVQ: industry control, rationalisation, knowledge and understanding, and key skills

9.22 It is important that the 800 NVQs should reflect the needs of the sector of industry for which they were designed. Consequently no recommendations have been made in this Report to change NVQ. In the proposed restructuring of the NCVQ and SCAA, the need for the contents of GNVQs to be related to NVQs has been recognised, as has the need for industry to retain control of the development of NVQs.

9.23 The NVQ relies for its rationale and success on its integration into industry and commerce, and effective control being exercised by line managers. The strong role played by consultants, personnel specialists and representatives of trade associations has been essential to get the NVQs launched. Perhaps the extent of the involvement of such specialists has been a factor in the complexity and specialised language of which some employers now complain. To build understanding, practising line managers now need to be fully involved in the formulation of the NVQ qualifications.

9.24 There are over 100 bodies accredited to offer NVQs, although two-thirds of them operate in partnership with one or other of the larger awarding bodies. Half of all NVQs are awarded by the City and Guilds of London Institute (CGLI). In contrast to A levels, NVQs are identical whoever administers them, but there are concerns that the quality and standards of assessment vary to an unacceptable extent, and it is often argued that fewer bodies should be involved. An employer wishing to secure qualifications for a range of employees in different occupations may find it necessary to deal with several different systems and procedures. Similarly, colleges can find themselves dealing with a number of different verifiers. The proposed recommendation in the Beaumont Report is that partnerships between awarding bodies and cross-recognition of approvals and procedures should be strengthened. I **recommend** that the NCVQ and the DfEE should work with awarding bodies to secure rational and coherent provision in the interests of customers of the system.

9.25 Employers generally consider that in practice the knowledge and understanding required for an NVQ are sufficiently covered, but they also believe that the specifications in the NVQs are not sufficiently clear. The latest NCVQ *Criteria and Guidance,* published in 1995, unequivocally states that knowledge and understanding have to be specified. More progress must be made in implementing this. The proposed rationalisation of existing vocational qualifications, bringing them into alignment with the 800 NVQs, will give an added impetus to this work.

9.26 The other major aspect of the NVQ that impinges on this Review is its coverage of the key skill in communication, the application of number and information technology. Full recommendations have been made on these needs in Section 7 of this Report.

The rigour of the GNVQ and the NVQ

9.27 The terms of reference for this Review placed emphasis on maintaining the rigour of A levels. Rigour (as defined in Section 10.2) is a characteristic no less required of the GNVQ and NVQ qualifications, although its application needs to reflect their different purposes and content. Both qualifications, especially the GNVQ, are at relatively early stages of development. There have been concerns about the extent to which they develop the knowledge and understanding needed for a subject, trade or profession, and also about the reliability of assessment. At the heart of the Review is a recognition of the centrality of applied and vocational education, and the need for both to be accorded the respect and esteem historically given to achievement in academic qualifications. This Review has therefore been concerned to: support the work of the NCVQ and the work of the Beaumont Review of NVQs and the Capey Review of GNVQs, the outcomes of which were recently reported (see Appendix G1 and G2); to learn from experience; and to strengthen the GNVQ and the NVQ. Stating the Government's commitment to vocational education in September 1995, the Prime Minister said:

> 'No-one should doubt the commitment I feel to reversing this country's historic weaknesses in vocational education, nor the determination which Gillian Shephard and I share to make the new qualifications work, not by glossing over the problems which do exist in some areas, but by rooting them out and instilling high quality courses with more rigorous testing and external marking.'

9.28 The Beaumont and Capey Reports which followed the Prime Minister's speech record widespread support for the GNVQ and the NVQ. The Capey Report says, for example:

> 'Respondents were very positive about the GNVQ philosophy and structure. It was seen as a much welcomed initiative that was meeting the needs of large numbers of students ...'

9.29 The Beaumont Report received wide evidence of support for the NVQ, with 80 per cent of respondents to consultation giving it their backing.

9.30 But both Beaumont and Capey Reviews found widespread criticism of implementation. The greatest concerns related to the whole business of assessment, and at the heart of this lies the need to establish assessment that is rigorous in the sense of being apt for its purpose, giving assurance of high and uniform standards across the country, and yet cost-effective. It is that balance which the NCVQ is striving to establish for both NVQs and GNVQs. To make that comment is a recognition of the difficulty of developing an approach that best meets the needs of a distinctive approach to learning, and develops qualities that employers value.

9.31 The distinctiveness of the NVQ has derived from the principle that candidates have to demonstrate mastery of a subject, trade or profession. Rigour in NVQs has meant that every detailed aspect of what is involved in mastery has to be demonstrated by the candidate, and assessed. Good performance in some aspects does not compensate for inadequate performance in others. The required standard has to be met in every specified element. This is different from the traditional form of assessment in the GCSE and A levels, which is based on sampling and allows for compensation in grading so that candidates may compensate for low achievement in one aspect of their work by high achievement in another. The concept of mastery is so fundamental to the NVQ that there are no grades of achievement: either there is mastery or there is not. Whatever criticisms have been made of the two qualifications, there is no ground for complaint that the assessment is other than thorough in its coverage. As the Beaumont Report says:

> 'Employers need to know their employees can actually do what is required of them. They cannot send a worker to someone's house who has only demonstrated the ability to perform some of the requirements. Employers' performance reviews check for total competence, irrespective of qualifications. NVQ/SVQ assessment is carried out over an extended period. It includes repeated demonstration.' (The Beaumont Report, Section 4.)

9.32 The GNVQ, unlike the NVQ, is graded and has external tests with a 70 per cent pass rate for all mandatory units. The scale of assessment, deriving from the mastery principle and the number of criteria for assessment, has become a treadmill for schools and colleges. The Capey Committee, analysing research reports, found widespread concern about the manageability of assessment. This was an issue that also arose frequently in the course of this Review. They also found problems with grading, core skills and external tests. Several of the reports referred to variability in standards, both of specification and verification.

9.33 Another concern, albeit one addressed by the NCVQ before the appointment of the Beaumont and Capey Committees, has been the basis of assessment. GNVQ assessment initially related more to the quality of the processes adopted by students in their work than to the quality of outcomes. That was addressed in September 1994, through the incorporation of 'Quality of Outcomes' in the grading criteria. Another concern has been the limited role of examinations and the quality of the arrangements for verifying the assessment of course work made by course leaders in institutions. Qualifications related to practical applications make much use of non-written assessment, and it is difficult to ensure that such assessment is to common national standards.

Action taken by the NCVQ to improve rigour

9.34 The NCVQ has already made a number of innovations to improve rigour. The content of the GNVQ and NVQ specifications stating what has to be assessed has been progressively enlarged to make it clearer. The context of assessment and evidence required in support of conclusions has been added to clarify what would be acceptable as evidence of attainment in the GNVQ. For example, more detail and exemplification of the knowledge and understanding required have been added to the GNVQ specifications to make the standards expected clearer.

9.35 As stated earlier, the 1995 issue of the NCVQ *Criteria and Guidance*, made clear the need for the specification of knowledge in the NVQs. Policies are being implemented to improve the quality of verification of NVQ assessments by the institutions. A common accord was established between the NCVQ and the NVQ awarding bodies on assessment and verification in 1993. The NCVQ has set up regional offices to monitor and provide advice on quality assurance. Improved standards for assessors and verifiers were published in 1994. The eventual target is for all assessors and verifiers to be formally qualified.

9.36 There are similar requirements for GNVQ assessors and verifiers to be qualified. NCVQ established a programme of work to improve the rigour of GNVQ assessment following a request from Mr Boswell, then Parliamentary Secretary to the Department for Education in early 1994[2]. The programme of work is now well under way. Among the outcomes anticipated are benchmark exemplar materials to aid assessment and verification, a document on external verifier training and practice, and a checklist of good practice in the design of assignments.

9.37 A number of further initiatives are now being piloted through the Part One GNVQ qualification. (See Section 9.11.) These are:

- The use of extension tests to assess the depth of understanding, and to contribute to decisions on whether to award a merit or distinction grade.

- The introduction of a controlled assignment, set by the awarding body, marked by teachers and remarked by the awarding body, as a means of standardising grading standards across the country.

- The provision of greater information to teachers on what is required, together with suggested approaches to teaching.

- A simple and direct approach to setting out specifications.

---

2   Mr Boswell's six point plan asked NCVQ to do the following to enhance the quality of GNVQs: clarify the knowledge and understanding required in GNVQ units; improve the assessment regime; review and clarify the basis for grading; extend training for external verifiers; provide more and clearer guidance for teachers; and tighten the criteria for accrediting schools and colleges.

9.38 Because the Part One GNVQ was designed for use in schools, its specifications include appropriate cross-references to the content of the National Curriculum, not least in relation to communication, the application of number, information technology, and those parts of the National Curriculum concerned with science and technology.

9.39 The inspectorates are evaluating the pilot of the Part One GNVQ. The NCVQ has made clear that it will monitor these innovations closely with a view, if they are successful and where they are relevant, to their extension across the GNVQ generally.

9.40 As mentioned elsewhere in this Report, an initiative is being taken by the regulatory bodies jointly, to simplify the terminology of qualifications and to adopt whenever possible a common vocabulary of terms. This will help institutions interpret what is required, and comply more effectively with national standards.

Changes to come

9.41 A qualification like the NVQ should not be granted unless a candidate has demonstrated all the competences necessary to provide a reliable service to a client. But the GNVQ is not a professional qualification: it covers a broad area of knowledge and understanding which underpins a range of trades and professions, and provides a basis for a practical education. The mastery model is therefore inappropriate to the GNVQ, so I welcome the proposal in the Capey Report that assessment should no longer cover every detail, but should be based on an overall assessment of performance in defined areas known as units. This will reduce workload and avoid the risk that assessment may become a burdensome series of atomistic assessments.

9.42 I also welcome the proposals in the Capey Report for simplifying grading criteria based on the two themes of process and quality of outcomes.

9.43 A more rigorous use of external assessment in the GNVQ is to be welcomed. It should reduce the overall burden of internal assessment and assure uniform standards. It will also help to exemplify the depth of understanding to be achieved. The Capey Committee proposes externally set assignments to contribute towards grading. Grading, it is recommended, should be based on an externally set assignment for one unit (or in exceptional cases, more than one unit) and on evidence from course work for a number of specified units.

9.44 The Capey Committee recommended that the NCVQ should look at the feasibility of using externally set and moderated standard assignments in a vocational context for the units in communication, the application of number and information technology. This will help improve the rigour of assessment, reduce its burden, and clarify the standard of work required. These assignments must, of course, validly assess the skills achieved and be cost-effective. Given the importance of consistency in standards to the credibility of key skills assessment, I also welcome NCVQ's willingness to look at the feasibility and value of external tests of components of the key skills.

9.45 The Capey Committee recommended that NCVQ and the Joint Council comprising the three awarding bodies should work towards tests common to City and Guilds, RSA, and BTEC. Because of concerns about the uneven quality of the tests, I **recommend** that consideration be given to a unified test approved by NCVQ in advance of use.

9.46 The Capey Committee has also recommended that the *purpose* of the existing external tests should be reviewed. I **recommend** that the role of these external tests should be reconsidered to determine whether candidates should be required to answer questions covering the entire range of knowledge specified in a mandatory unit, whether the tests should be graded, and if so, the basis of grading. This review of the external tests should take account of what has been learned from the use of tests in the Part One GNVQ pilot, and in particular the extent to which they test the depth of understanding.

9.47 Until the development of the Part One GNVQ, the tests were solely to judge whether students' knowledge and understanding covered the whole range of what was required. If the use of tests to contribute to grading is validated through the Part One GNVQ pilot, I **recommend** that that is one of the purposes for which they should be used. This would require testing depth of understanding and moving away from reliance exclusively on multiple choice questions. Higher levels of understanding are probably best assessed in other ways, requiring more extended answers than the selection of an answer offered in a multiple choice test. I am glad to record that the NCVQ and SCAA have decided that alternatives to multiple choice questions should be explored as part of the Part One GNVQ pilot. Since the quality of assessment is fundamental to the long-term success of the GNVQ, some increase in costs should be accepted if this proves to be necessary to ensure quality.

9.48 The Part One GNVQ pilot has expanded the information available to teachers through explanatory notes on the GNVQ specifications. The NCVQ has now decided that this should be taken further, to provide a specification of the required knowledge and understanding. I **recommend** that this practice should be extended (where it would be helpful) across the GNVQ generally, and that SCAA, ACAC and CCEA should support this work.

9.49 For the NVQ, the Beaumont Committee argues that the quality of assessment needs to be improved and the cost reduced. It points to 'much justified criticism of assessment and verification', and reports considerable evidence that candidates, assessors and verifiers are uncertain about the consistency and accuracy of assessment. As stated in 9.25 above, there are still concerns about the way in which what is to be assessed is written. Knowledge and understanding in particular may be marginalised and overlooked if they are not well specified.

9.50 In response to these concerns, the Committee advises that a combination of approaches to assessment (including external assessment) is needed to provide a rigorous approach. Different combinations will be needed for different qualifications and levels.

9.51 The Committee recommends research to develop an assessment model, to be completed in April 1996. In the light of this, the NCVQ and its sister body, the Scottish Vocational Education Council (SCOTVEC) should issue guidance on the selection of assessment methods and approve the assessment methods used by awarding bodies, as part of accrediting their work. As the Beaumont Report argues 'there must be an over-riding requirement to demonstrate rigour' (see Beaumont Report, Section 4, paragraph 4.1).

9.52 Sir Michael Heron, the Chairman of the NCVQ, welcomes this approach and the proposals made to improve the quality, verification and cost-effectiveness of assessment. We see external verification and the training of external verifiers as fundamental to confidence in the system of NVQs, coupled with greater clarity in the statements of what is required of a candidate to justify an award. As NCVQ already recognises, NVQs must make clear what someone should know and understand as well as the outcomes they must achieve.

National data on GNVQs and NVQs

9.53 Changes are being made at a national level to improve the quality of data available on GNVQs and NVQs. I welcome these changes which, when implemented, should provide reliable information about take-up, wastage, and completions and contribute to judgements about the rigour of these qualifications.

9.54 The DfEE has set up a database for GNVQs which will be fully operational in October 1996. It will standardise the data collected by the awarding bodies and allow tracking of individuals. Among other things, it will be possible to establish who is still on a course, who has gained an award, who has changed courses, and who has left.

9.55 The Beaumont Report has asked NCVQ to make it clear to awarding bodies what information should be made available. NCVQ will be working with the awarding bodies on how best to standardise the methods for collecting and presenting data on NVQs.

Other vocational qualifications: Improving coherence

9.56 There are three other major and related concerns that call for national action to improve the coherence of the qualifications framework in relation to vocational qualifications so that access to and progression from one qualification to another can be greatly improved.

9.57 These concerns are about:

- The relationship between GNVQs and NVQs.

- The needs of those who are not able to demonstrate competence in the workplace.

- The role of existing vocational qualifications other than NVQs and GNVQs.

9.58 In the White Paper, *Competitiveness: Forging Ahead* (Cm 2867, 1995), the Government invited the NCVQ to consider the need for the skills, knowledge and understanding that underpin an NVQ to be certificated separately, to facilitate access to the NVQ qualification for those not able to demonstrate competence in the workplace. In some cases, this is done currently through arrangements with colleges and other education providers, sometimes using older, knowledge-based, vocational qualifications. The NCVQ has recommended that these arrangements should be rationalised by expressing the outcomes of such education or training as GNVQ additional units. There are advantages in this approach. It would build on existing strengths; it would harness the resources of the extended network of colleges of further education; it would bring greater coherence into the world of qualifications; and it would also go a long way to respond to concerns expressed that the NVQ does not adequately provide candidates with the knowledge and understanding needed to translate everyday competence into the capability to deal with unfamiliar problems encountered at work.

9.59 There are currently ten GNVQs, each available at three levels. Five have been available from September 1993, three from 1994 and two from September of this year. Two further qualifications are planned for introduction from September 1996, one in 1997 and two more in 1998 making a total of 15. Information from NCVQ indicates that there has been substantial take-up of these qualifications. This should be seen in the context of continued wide take-up of other existing vocational qualifications and the 800 qualifications available in the NVQ family.

9.60 Table Six shows the estimated number of 16–18 year olds undertaking different types of Advanced level vocational courses in schools and further education colleges in England in 1993/94 and 1994/95. Though it is perhaps too early to identify trends, this table shows a significant increase in the number of young people undertaking Advanced GNVQs, and a substantial decrease in the number of young people undertaking non-GNVQ Advanced courses.

Table 6 16–18 year olds undertaking Advanced level vocational courses in schools and further education colleges (England)[3]

	Schools 1993/94	Schools 1994/95	Colleges 1993/94	Colleges 1994/95
Advanced GNVQ	4 300 (41%)	13 300 (78%)	20 900 (15%)	52 800 (38%)
BTEC National/ C&G DVE (National)	6 100 (57%)	3 400 (20%)	109 900 (78%)	76 600 (55%)
NVQ Level 3	200 (2%)	300 (2%)	10 400 (7%)	9 100 (7%)
Total	10 600	17 000	141 200	138 500

9.61 The table also shows that the number of young people in further education colleges taking vocational awards other than the GNVQ and the NVQ in 1994/95 was still large. Recent data on student provision published by FEFC[4] shows that the number of such awards is very large for students above the age of 19. In 1994/95, 74% of those studying for Advanced level vocational qualifications in further education (353,000 out of 475,000) were undertaking qualifications other than NVQs and GNVQs. Some 400,000 students were pursuing vocational qualifications other than GNVQs and NVQs at levels 1 and Entry level, and 218,000 at level 2 (Intermediate).

9.62 Information from the Further Education Development Agency (FEDA) indicates that:

- In some sectors (for example engineering and photography) college lecturers would prefer to continue with BTEC Nationals as these have status in the industry.

- Some college lecturers believe that GNVQs provide a very broad area of study at a point where many students may wish to develop some specialisms.

---

3   1993/94 estimates taken from DfEE Statistical Bulletin 10/94, Table 10; 1994/95 estimates supplied by DfEE Analytical Services Branch.

4   Taken from "Student Numbers in the Further Education Sector in England in 1994-95," FEFC, January 1996

- This is perceived to be more of an issue at Advanced level than at Intermediate and Foundation levels.

- Because of their lack of specialisation, GNVQs may be less appropriate for adult learners.

- Colleges also want to retain BTEC Nationals, as NVQs are increasingly being delivered via work-based routes (see the Beaumont Report).

9.63 One of the main themes in this Review has been the need for coherence. But the overriding requirement is that the needs of students, trainees, apprentices and employers should be met. This means that while the policy that vocational qualifications should be absorbed into the NVQ and GNVQ families is right and should be pursued, the other qualifications should stand until there is a replacement for them. There are legitimate claims that some of the existing qualifications cater for needs that are not presently met, either by an NVQ that requires the candidate to have access to relevant employment, or by the broadly-based GNVQ.

9.64 Precisely how existing qualifications outside the NVQ and GNVQ can be brought into the main framework is still to be determined, but I would expect many of them to be mapped on to NVQ and GNVQ, to make clear to users how they fit with NVQ assessment and how they could add to GNVQ.

9.65 I **recommend** that NCVQ in conjunction with the vocational awarding bodies, should pursue the following proposals for increasing coherence in the field of school and college-based vocational training:

- Map existing qualifications, for which there is substantial demand, on to GNVQs and NVQs to identify areas of overlap or close relationship.

- Increase the pool of optional and additional units of GNVQs to allow for greater specialisation.

- Consider greater flexibility in the structure of GNVQs, for example by reducing the number of mandatory units required in those awards without compromising comparability.

- Take into account the implications of the proposal for six-unit awards based on the full GNVQ at Advanced level outlined elsewhere in this Report.

- Consider the need for full GNVQs in new areas.

- Look for ways of certificating existing qualifications as part of an NVQ or GNVQ.

9.66 Nevertheless a range of awards will continue outside this framework, often in response to the desire for locally customised provision which meets the requirements of particular groups of learners or employees. Much of this provision is accredited through the Open College Networks (OCNs) which provide a thorough quality assurance system and progression routes to national awards. I **recommend** that links should be developed between the regulatory bodies and the National Open College Network to ensure that OCN accreditation leads to complementary local provision rather than a replication of national awards.

SECTION 10

A levels

Part I: The rigour of A levels

10.1 The Interim Report in July posed seven questions to do with the rigour of A levels.

- Are A levels in different subjects all at the same standard?

- Should A level syllabuses make the required outcomes more explicit as the vocational qualifications do?

- Does the continual small annual rise in the average level of achievement in AS and A levels in recent years imply a rise in performance or an easing of standards?

- Does the large number of different AS and A level options available for some popular subjects militate against the maintenance of uniform standards?

- Are modular AS and A levels as demanding as conventional AS and A levels with a single final examination?

- Should the requirement for synoptic assessment, which at present only applies to the modular AS and A levels, be extended to conventional terminal examinations?

- Are concerns about levels of achievement (and take-up) in mathematics and the sciences well-founded, and if so, what action should be taken?

10.2 I start by considering the first six issues, with 'rigour' being defined as follows:

> '(that) the level of demand on students should be maintained; that requirements are clear; that assessments by awarding bodies should be to common national standards; that assessment should be firmly based, fit for its purpose and consistent over time, with checks to ensure that standards are being maintained.' (Interim Report, Section 7.2)

10.3 The recommendations in this Section of the Report take account of the views expressed in consultation, a survey conducted for the Review, and further studies undertaken by the School Curriculum and Assessment Authority (SCAA), and the Curriculum and Assessment Authority for Wales (ACAC) into comparability between different A level syllabuses, subjects and schemes of assessment.

Consultation

10.4 Views expressed during consultation endorsed the importance of maintaining the rigour of A levels. Employers and those in higher education, as well as students and their parents, want to be sure that the standards associated with A levels are secure and that where choices are involved (for example between different syllabuses or boards), fairness and consistency of treatment are assured. Though there was support for choice between syllabuses, there was also general agreement that a reduction in the number of syllabuses, especially in the major subjects where there are many choices, would contribute to the maintenance of consistent standards. Some respondents pointed out that a perceived variation in standards between boards is also an issue which needs to be reviewed, and many in the education sector perceive there to be a variation in standards between subjects, which is not desirable.

10.5 There was wide support for the positive aspects of modularity in A levels (for example, in terms of motivation), and nearly half of the total sample survey (46 per cent) commented on aspects of modularity. Few chose to comment on the requirement, for the final unit in modular A levels, to include questions involving a synoptic coverage of the whole content of an A level, and only a few supported its extension to conventional A levels. Many would argue that since the end of course examinations in conventional A levels sample the whole of the syllabus, they are already "synoptic" and that this is therefore only an issue for modular A levels.

10.6 Some scepticism was expressed about the feasibility of coming to a judgement on whether standards have changed over time. There was, however, general support for making the required outcomes more explicit in A levels, as in vocational qualifications.

Studies carried out by SCAA and ACAC

10.7 In support of this Review, a detailed programme of work was undertaken by SCAA and ACAC into the comparability and rigour of various components of the A level examination system. Many of the issues examined are inter-related.

10.8 In addition to discussions with the awarding bodies and other users of qualifications, the following work was carried out:

- Analysis of the Department for Education and Employment (DfEE) 16+/18+ national examinations results database to investigate the relationship between performance in different A level subjects.

- Use of the Universities and Colleges Admissions Service (UCAS) databases to investigate the relationship between subject difficulty and higher education entry requirements.

- Identification of the ways in which some A level syllabuses currently make the outcomes explicit.

- A "standards over time" project in England being carried out jointly by SCAA with the Office for Standards in Education (OFSTED) to see if these have changed.

- Desk research to analyse the comparability of standards, assisted by SCAA's scrutiny reports on A level examining in recent years.

- A descriptive exercise to show the range of syllabus options in a few key subjects.

- An investigation of the comparability across awarding bodies in two subjects, one with many options (history) and one with few options (economics).

- An investigation of the preferred timing for institutions of modular examinations, carried out by Market and Opinion Research International (MORI).

■ A detailed investigation of the comparability of standards in 'old' modular syllabuses with those in corresponding linear syllabuses. (Modular syllabuses have only been generally available for a short period.) The subjects considered were English, mathematics and the sciences.

■ A desk exercise to summarise approaches to synoptic assessment in A levels.

10.9 A summary of this work is to be found in the two Review Reports referred to in Appendix A1.

10.10 I now turn to:

■ Comparability between subjects (Section 10.11-10.21).

■ Comparability between awarding bodies and between syllabuses (Section 10.22-10.37).

■ Comparability of standards over time (Section 10.38-10.44).

■ Comparability between modular and traditional linear A levels[1] (Section 10.45-10.61).

■ Making outcomes more explicit in A levels (Section 10.62-10.65).

Comparability between subjects

10.11 Studies by SCAA (using procedures developed by Newcastle University's A level Information System – ALIS) suggest that A levels differ between subjects in the level of demand made of students and in their grading. In these studies, factors have been computed for three successive national cohorts of A level students (1993–1995) to assess the adjustments that would need to be made for each A level subject in order to equate the subjects for difficulty. (See Appendix G3.)

10.12 The basis of these studies is a comparison between grades earned in the General Certificate of Secondary Education (GCSE) and those in A levels. Taking the students' overall performance in the GCSE as the baseline, a highly graded performance in the GCSE not matched by a highly graded performance in a specific A level would suggest that the standard required in that particular A level is more demanding than in another subject where the A level outcome, for the same level of performance in the GCSE, is better. This is a simplified statement of the approach, but it indicates the broad lines.

10.13 The conclusion that emerges from such studies is that there are apparent differences in subject difficulty at A level. There is a group of 'difficult' subjects which includes physical sciences and mathematics, economics, history, German, French and general studies. There is a group of 'average difficulty' subjects which includes biology, computer studies, geography, religious studies and Spanish. A group of 'easier than average subjects' includes business studies, classical studies, home economics, design and technology, English, and communication studies. (Comments on music and art are not offered because the methodology may not be appropriate to these subjects since talent in them is not necessarily closely related to achievement in the generality of GCSE subjects.)

---

[1] This section refers also to synoptic assessment.

10.14 The first issue is whether this analysis is valid. That needs to be debated.

10.15 Some may contend that even though it is valid, the differences are long standing, and providing universities are aware of inter-subject differences in grading standards, no action is required. Universities will fill places on some ranking order within subject specialisms, and generally admissions tutors will take this factor into account. While there is force in this argument, it relies on a sophistication in university admissions procedures that may be doubted to exist, given the large number of decisions that have to be taken in a highly diverse system in a period of a few weeks. Moreover, not all A level students go to university, and employers cannot be expected to know the subject differentials. Finally, a principle of equity suggests that students should receive equal recognition for equal achievement, and any biasing of student choice of subjects by differential standards would serve no good purpose.

10.16 For these reasons, subjects should consistently relate awards to achievement. The next step is for the awarding bodies to consider the evidence, assess the validity of the conclusion to which it appears to lead, and discuss their conclusions with the regulatory bodies.

10.17 If the outcome of these studies were to be confirmed by further work, and if the differences were significant, there would be four possible courses of action:

■ Level down the difficulty of the most demanding subjects.

■ Raise the level of the easiest subjects.

■ A combination of both.

■ Publicise the differences but take no action in assessment and reporting terms.

10.18 An answer is not as straightforward as it may seem. The third option, which seems the most obvious, would mean lowering standards in mathematics, the physical sciences and some modern foreign languages. These are subjects where there is particular concern in the universities that preparation at A level needs attention. There would be opposition therefore to any lowering of grading standards in these subjects.

10.19 A general raising of standards to those of the most demanding subjects would increase failure rates. Already 30% of those beginning on a programme of two A levels do not achieve them. Raising standards quickly would exacerbate that problem.

10.20 But as stated in Section 10.15, there are practical reasons for seeking parity in standards. This would point to raising the required standard in the apparently less demanding subjects to the average level, even though that might reduce the number choosing to take A levels. Since there are now the alternatives of General National Vocational Qualifications (GNVQs) and Modern Apprenticeships in the work-based route, which offer a different form of challenge and have been found to be highly motivating, we should be encouraging more students to consider these options.

10.21 I **recommend** that:

■ There should be no reduction in the standards required in any subject.

■ The awarding bodies should review the evidence prepared for this Report and reach agreed conclusions with the regulatory bodies. Where subjects seem decidedly below the 'average' level of difficulty, there should be a levelling-up of demand, after giving advance warning to institutions. Details of the procedure for bringing about this change should be agreed between the regulatory and awarding bodies and be subject to the approval of the Secretaries of State.

Comparability between awarding bodies and between syllabuses

10.22 The issue of comparability between awarding bodies and between syllabuses arises for two main reasons:

■ Some concerns have been expressed that schools 'shop around' between awarding bodies to take advantage of A level syllabuses which are thought to be 'easier' than others.

■ The sheer number of syllabuses, and in some cases, options within syllabuses, makes it difficult to ensure that there are consistent standards.

10.23 Taking these in turn, it is the case that many schools choose different examination boards from time to time. It is this practice that gives rise to publicly-expressed concern.

10.24 Schools do have legitimate reasons for this action. With a range of syllabuses available, subject departments in institutions review them to see which will provide the greatest opportunities to adopt an approach to a subject which students will find most worthwhile in terms of interest, challenge and coverage. An enthusiasm by teaching staff is material to the quality of the learning experience they offer to students. It makes for good education.

10.25 Nevertheless, in an era of competition for students between institutions, and with the annual publication of performance tables, as well as a touch of competition between awarding bodies, it is right that the community at large should look for reassurance that standards are both consistent within a subject, and are not being depreciated by the competitive forces at work.

10.26 The responsibility for ensuring that there is one consistently applied standard lies with regulatory and awarding bodies. I **recommend** that:

■ The awarding bodies should ensure that standards are equivalent through their internal and collective procedures.

■ The regulatory bodies should have the final responsibility to ensure that all is well.

■ Each school and college should have a formal procedure, involving the head/principal of the institution, before a decision is taken to change an awarding body.

10.27 Turning to the second aspect of comparability of standards (the number of syllabuses), the task of ensuring equal standards is particularly difficult when the number of syllabuses available across the awarding bodies is large.

Table 7 A level and AS Syllabuses[2] in English, Mathematics and the Sciences[3]

	Linear	Modular	Total
English	27	14	41
Mathematics	32	67	99
Sciences	41	66	107

10.28 The number of modular syllabuses, as illustrated in the table, adds to the magnitude of the problem.

10.29 The provision of alternatives within syllabuses also places a considerable strain on the available resources of awarding bodies.

10.30 A review of 41 reports from SCAA's scrutinies of A levels carried out in 1993 and 1994 showed that more than half of the reports raised concerns about comparability across options in a syllabus. During that period, there were also nine reports comparing the way in which awarding bodies examined a particular subject. In all of these, concerns were raised about the inconsistency of demand across optional routes.

10.31 In a detailed analysis of the options available within one awarding body's A level history syllabus, over half the candidature was accounted for by three of the 30 options. Nine options had fewer than ten candidates each. The grades awarded in each option varied considerably.

10.32 Despite an intensive programme of scrutinies, comparability studies, question-paper reviews, and probes carried out by SCAA and ACAC, only some 10 per cent of syllabuses and examinations are monitored closely each year. Syllabuses within a particular subject and awarding body cannot, on average, even be scrutinised once every five years with present resources.

10.33 The current balance between providing a range of syllabuses large enough to reflect the different curriculum approaches used in schools and colleges, and small enough to assure high quality examinations of a uniform standard, needs reconsideration. There is a strong case for reducing syllabus numbers in a controlled and systematic way to improve the quality of examinations and to enable a more comprehensive monitoring programme to be carried out.

10.34 SCAA conducted a detailed review of GCSE results in mathematics and science in 1994. This involved a thorough examination of scripts, prompted by doubts arising from a distinct rise in the number of B grades awarded by two awarding bodies. Since then, arrangements to ensure consistency of standards across boards have been

---

[2] It is difficult to produce definitive syllabus numbers because there is no generally accepted definition of a syllabus. Moreover, separate syllabuses can be closely related, for example, through common examination papers for A and AS awards, or through the same syllabus content being examined in different ways, which means that problems of comparability between syllabuses do not always arise.

[3] Each of these titles covers a range of A levels (eg 'the Sciences' include biology and chemistry, physics, science, environmental science, geology, electronics and psychology). In English and mathematics there is also a range of titles.

strengthened at both GCSE and A level. These procedures need to be kept under review, and I draw attention to the recommendation in Section 10.44 that there should be an in-depth quinquennial review of standards across the awarding bodies in all subjects, to supplement the annual checks.

10.35 Reducing the numbers of syllabuses and options alone, however, will not necessarily improve the consistency of examinations. There is evidence from studies by the regulatory bodies to suggest that many of the difficulties associated with comparability stem from the quality of individual questions, the balance of questions within the paper and the mark schemes. The resources saved by reducing syllabus and option numbers could be diverted towards training and support programmes for senior examiners. An examination is only as good as the questions and mark schemes from which it is built up.

10.36 Consideration should therefore be given to the appropriateness of the current balance within the programme of work of the regulatory bodies in terms of regulation, monitoring and support. They should play a more significant role in terms of training and support, through the expansion of the senior examiners' conference programme and the commissioning of research into setting effective questions and papers. The role of pre-testing of examination questions should be considered further with the awarding bodies.

10.37 I recommend that:

- The regulatory bodies, working in partnership with the awarding bodies, should reduce the number of syllabuses and options to levels where it is practical for them to be satisfied that equal standards prevail without requiring an unreasonable level of resources for the task, while preserving a reasonable choice for centres.

- With a reduction in the number of syllabuses and options, the resources thus released should be devoted to ensuring consistency of standards.

- The Secretaries of State should consider implementing Section 24 of the 1988 Education Reform Act which allows them to approve qualifications and a designated body to approve syllabuses. Implementation would give the designated regulatory body the power to control the number of syllabuses and content, if needed.

Comparability of standards over time: the implications for standards of the small annual rise in student achievements in AS and A levels

10.38 During recent years, candidates' performance in A levels has been rising as Table 8 shows:

Table 8 A level pass rates (grades A – E across all subjects 1989-1995

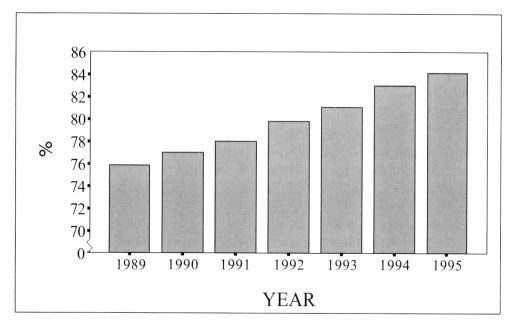

10.39 There has been a similar pattern in the GCSE.

10.40 This rise, when linked to the increasing numbers taking these examinations, has prompted questions as to whether the rise in achievement reflects improvements in teaching and a rising level of achievement by students, or whether it reflects a depreciation of the standards of the qualification.

10.41 The Secretary of State for Education and Employment agreed that OFSTED and SCAA should proceed with proposals for a review of examination standards at 16+ and 18+ over the past twenty years in England. The subjects chosen were English, mathematics and science (chemistry). The work was conducted with the help of the GCSE and GCE boards. I had hoped that the results of this work would be available in time for this Report, but more needs to be done before a final report will be available.

10.42 Such a study, which involves a detailed review of syllabuses, examination papers and other material, depends on the availability of archive material on a range of subjects over a long run of years. It also means taking account of the effects over the years of changes in the balance of syllabus content. Unfortunately the availability of archive material has proved to be limited, and this has made the task of the independent specialists who have been engaged in the work particularly difficult.

10.43 I think it better to allow further time for this work than to attempt to draw tentative conclusions at this stage. During the wider consultation in this Review, views have however been expressed by universities on mathematics, which have been sufficiently clear to lead to recommendations for action. These are reported in Section 10, Part II, on mathematics and the sciences.

10.44 Meanwhile I make the following **recommendations** to ensure that there is a basis and accepted procedure in the future for monitoring and safeguarding standards over time.

- The awarding bodies should maintain a comprehensive archive of examination papers, scripts, mark schemes, coursework, examination statistics and awards so that there is a better basis than at present to assess standards over time. The basis of this archive should be agreed between the regulatory and awarding bodies.

- Similar archives for checking standards over time should be set up for GNVQs, taking into account their distinctive characteristics, and what it would be feasible to retain and the effects on schools and colleges. The basis of this archive should be agreed between the awarding bodies and NCVQ.

- In addition to the annual checks of standards, the regulatory bodies (in association with the awarding bodies) should undertake an in-depth review of standards, so that over five years all subjects are covered, to ensure that standards are being maintained over time and across boards.

Comparability between modular and traditional linear A levels

Background to the debate

10.45 Over recent years, and particularly since 1995, schools have been able to choose between offering the traditional linear A levels, in which typically the largest proportion of the marks depends on a single final examination, or modular A levels in which examinations and marks may be spread over up to six modules.

10.46 Within education, modularity has been warmly welcomed and supported. It has been widely adopted by universities, and its general availability in schools and colleges has followed university practice. Its proponents produce a long list of advantages, as follows.

- The motivation that comes from achievement.

- The diagnostic value of information from the early results, especially for part-time adult students.

- The motivation to students to maintain a high commitment to their work as a result of the prospect of examinations throughout the course. In the traditional linear A level, by contrast, there is a tendency for some to take life easy in the first year.

- The opportunity to have achievement recognised if, for personal or career reasons, studies are interrupted, and the associated opportunity to resume studies in another part of the country if there has been a move of home.

- In principle, modularity provides the basis for credit accumulation and transfer, between institutions and possibly between programmes.

- Modularity gives an opportunity to resit a module and achieve, on merit, a better result through additional work.

■ A spread of modular assessments is likely to give a fairer and more accurate reading of a candidate's achievements than a single terminal examination where everything turns on performance over a very short period of time in relation to one set of papers. Modular assessment is more valid than the single sample of a final examination.

10.47 Research conducted for the Review into the perceptions of A level and GNVQ students (see Appendix B4), indicated that both groups said that they believed a modular structure, together with assessed coursework, tested knowledge and reflected ability most fairly. Assessment procedures were of particular concern to the study participants. There was some indication that they thought end of course examinations were more adept at testing the ability to take exams than at measuring knowledge and understanding.

10.48 However, critics of modularity remain concerned that for two reasons, which do not derive from the achievements of the candidate, the modular approach will give higher results than the linear.

■ The availability of resits.

■ The absence of the major challenge represented by the traditional linear A level to master and use effectively in a final examination all the skills, knowledge and understanding achieved over the whole programme. Responding to that challenge is a major achievement by a candidate taking two, three or four A levels at the same time, and such achievement is greater than that of candidates following the modular route whose assessment is spread over 18 months or more.

10.49 A much fuller list of the strengths and weaknesses of modular A levels offered during the consultation for this Review is given in Appendix G4.

Monitoring of modularity by SCAA and ACAC

10.50 Whichever scheme of assessment is adopted, the A level is governed by rules promulgated by the regulatory bodies. Under these rules, all modules must be at the full A level standard, with no allowance being made for the relative immaturity in the subject of a student taking modules at an early stage of the course. The regulatory bodies have also prescribed that at least 30 per cent of the marks must be reserved for a final examination, and that the assessment must include questions which demand a synoptic knowledge of the whole of the required content of the A level.

10.51 Some 246 modular AS and A levels are now available out of a total of 465 AS and A level syllabuses, and take-up has been rapid. The work of the regulatory bodies (in collaboration with the awarding bodies), particularly over the next two years, will be fundamental to the maintenance of standards. So that there can be confidence that standards are not at risk, their findings and the basis for them should be made available for public scrutiny.

10.52 At this stage we have not had the first full two years of examinations of the new modules. These outcomes will not be available until late 1996 when they will be subject to detailed review by the regulatory and awarding bodies. Meanwhile SCAA and ACAC have been reviewing a sample of the papers and outcomes from the early modules in English, mathematics, biology, chemistry and physics. It would be premature to reach any conclusions until the first full cycle is completed, but at this stage a number of points are worth noting:

■ A tendency towards shorter or more structured questions in modular examinations.

■ More comprehensive syllabus coverage.

■ In some subjects, a relative absence of more demanding material to discriminate between the performance of those attaining the highest grades.

■ Some concern that it will prove difficult to avoid predictability in future question papers.

10.53 In 1995, an analysis of the previous summer's modular examination results in 13 subjects against their corresponding traditional linear syllabuses showed that the students taking the modular route gained higher average point scores in most subjects. Those syllabuses have now been superseded, but there was little evidence to suggest that a major contributory factor was any difference in grading standards in the two systems. SCAA and ACAC are continuing their review as examination papers and marks become available.

10.54 In the absence of complete sets of results for the first of the recently approved modular A levels, the most relevant matter for consideration is whether there are any intrinsic reasons to think that A level results are likely to improve as a result of modularity; if so, whether this represents a real lifting of achievement; and what implications there may be for the future of the linear A level.

10.55 In one respect, it is clear that, all other things being equal, the modular approach is likely to lead to candidates earning higher grades. This lies in the opportunity for candidates who are not satisfied with a mark to resit a module, or several modules, and not 'cash in' the result for a final award until they choose. Students are taking this opportunity. Candidates for the traditional linear A level will attempt resits less frequently, because it means resitting the whole examination, although coursework marks can be carried over. The evidence available shows that retaking in linear examinations is primarily a feature of lower-attaining candidates, while in modular examinations it is less restricted to this section of the cohort. It follows that resitting will tend to cause an even greater difference between the grade profiles of the two systems.

10.56 Proponents of the modular approach hold that this opportunity to improve grades is to be welcomed on the grounds that although candidates have taken advantage of the opportunity to resit, they have earned a higher mark by raising the quality of their work. They argue it is right that candidates should be encouraged to do more work and realise the benefit.

10.57 On the scale of the challenge represented by the final examination in the traditional linear route, the advocates of modularity contend that it places too much store on factual recall and memory of a kind not often required in life once examinations are over. They contend that the store of facts and arguments built up for the final examination soon fades and therefore has little long-term value: it is a largely pointless achievement. The advocates of the linear route counter that in life people are from time to time required to master and hold in their memory a great deal of information. Life involves facing major challenges which require sustained effort and endurance, characteristics that are tested by the traditional linear A level.

A response to the issues

10.58 These issues have been subject to extensive debate during the Review. There is no doubt of the breadth and strength of support for modularity at all levels in education. But if students generally prefer the modular approach, and if it is the case that, all other things being equal, the modular route produces better results, it could be that over a number of years the linear route will largely wither away.

10.59 The traditional linear A level has stood the test of 45 years. A far higher proportion of the cohort of young people is now successfully pursuing this route than was ever dreamt of when A levels were introduced. Modularity has a great deal in its favour, but there are, for want of a better word, enthusiasms in education for one approach or another, and dangers in an 'enthusiasm' becoming the universal practice, before the full consequences have been digested and evaluated. That process of evaluation takes years. I would therefore advise caution about encouraging or permitting a wholesale change to the modular route, for the following reasons.

- We are not yet clear about the effect on school and college management and learning of an A level system committed over the whole subject range to almost continuous external examination. It may be burdensome for schools, distracting for candidates, and damage the quality of learning. Particular concerns have been expressed about the different patterns of examination sessions that have emerged for modular examinations in different boards and the increasing complexity of examination schedules.

- It is not certain that it will be feasible in closely focused A level courses to produce a series of fresh questions for each module, so as to avoid predictability of questions.

- We have not yet developed an adequate and uniform approach to the intentionally demanding requirement to demonstrate a synoptic understanding of the whole coverage of the A level syllabus in modular schemes.

- Subjects lend themselves differentially to the modular approach. Some, like modern foreign languages, in which there is a close integration and relevance to each part of all that is learnt, do not seem suitable for assessment at the full A level standard until well into the course. In others, like English and history, the point during the course at which the assessment takes place makes a difference to the quality of the students' response to examination questions. In mathematics, where modularity has been practised for several years, there appear to be fewer problems, but the development of ability in algebraic manipulation and an underlying development of mathematical thinking must have some bearing on achievement. This raises two issues: differences between subjects, and the feasibility of questions being at the same level of demand in all modules. The second of these relates to the possibility that early modules should receive a lower weighting than modules taken at the end of the course. This is touched on in Section 11 on the reformulated AS.

- The traditional final examination is a demanding test and those who do well in it have a substantial achievement to their credit which universities and employers have learnt to respect.

10.60 Balancing the considerations we might do well to consider a different approach for the longer term. There may be advantage in seeking to combine the merits of both the traditional and modular A levels into a unified approach. This might typically involve a structure of three modules accounting for the first half the syllabus, and a final examination covering the remaining half, which would also include questions that test understanding of the syllabus as a whole. In practice, the first three modules would constitute the reformulated AS proposed in Section 11, while the final examination would assess the whole of the A level syllabus in greater depth. But that would be a substantial policy change.

10.61 I recommend that:

■ The regulatory bodies should monitor closely the comparability and consistency of standards in modular and traditional linear A levels and publish an annual report on this.

■ Consideration should be given to the approach outlined in Section 10.60, which, if the take-up of the traditional linear A level declines sharply, might become a standard form for A levels in the longer term.

■ In the meantime, both linear and modular A levels should be retained, but:

☐ the final examination in a modular scheme of assessment should count for not less than 30 per cent of the total marks and should include a number of questions, for which at least half the marks (15 per cent of the total marks for the A level) are reserved, that test understanding of the syllabus as a whole. (No changes are recommended for the traditional linear A level in this respect);

☐ there should be a limit on the number of resits of any one module, to be determined by the regulatory bodies after consultation with the awarding bodies;

☐ the regulatory bodies should monitor closely whether it is possible to maintain a stream of fresh questions for modular examinations to avoid easy question-spotting, particularly in early modules;

☐ the joint committee of the NCVQ and SCAA, with the involvement of Wales and Northern Ireland, should consider whether there should be a common timetable for modular examinations, based on two sittings a year, probably in January and June. They should consider this issue in consultation with the awarding bodies, considering at the same time the timing of GNVQ tests.

Making outcomes more explicit in A Levels[4]

10.62 The Interim Report posed the question whether A level syllabuses should make the required learning outcomes more explicit, as the vocational qualifications do. Response in consultation was generally supportive, with a number of caveats on the need for simplicity and manageability.

10.63 Work carried out by SCAA and ACAC on a number of approved A level syllabuses indicates the following conclusions.

- Few A level syllabuses require candidates to demonstrate specific outcomes other than the accumulation of marks, before a grade is awarded. However, the introduction of A level "subject cores", and other provisions such as a Code of Practice, have all caused syllabuses to be much more explicit about what is to be assessed, what will be rewarded, and how.

- Subject cores (which exist in many but not all subjects) provide a description of the syllabus knowledge, understanding and skills required of candidates, but on their own they do not make the outcomes explicit in relation to grades awarded.

- Syllabuses contain aims, assessment objectives, schemes of assessment and specified content, but the degree of specificity varies across subjects. Where there is a clear relationship between assessment objectives and assessment components, it may be possible to provide component grades in addition to an overall subject grade.

- Grade descriptions are not required by the Code of Practice for A levels, and are little used. Where they are used, they provide only a tenuous link between performance and explicit outcomes, since awarding decisions are made at component level, whereas grade descriptions almost always exist at subject level.

- Materials supporting syllabuses, such as published mark schemes and chief examiners' reports, provide more detail about the features associated with candidates' performance, but they provide little information about the explicit outcomes required of candidates.

10.64 It will be clear from the above that a variety of means exists currently within A level syllabuses to make outcomes more explicit, although the extent to which they do so in practice is inconsistent. While there is scope for making outcomes more explicit through further development of current procedures, to require students to achieve a minimum mark or grade in each component of the examination, before an overall subject grade could be awarded, would not be widely supported. Nevertheless, in view of the considerable support for greater convergence between A levels and Advanced GNVQs in these respects, further work is appropriate. In particular, the regulatory bodies should consider, with the awarding bodies, the scope for making outcomes more explicit in A levels through the defined subject cores, and the use of grade descriptions and component grades linked to specific assessment objectives.

10.65 **I recommend** that the regulatory bodies should examine the extent to which it is practical and advantageous to take further the specification of A levels in terms of required learning outcomes.

---

[4] At its simplest this is taken to mean making clear the knowledge, understanding and skills candidates will be expected to demonstrate for the award of a certificate or particular grade.

Part II: Mathematics and the sciences

The problem

10.66 The Interim Report referred to concerns about the declining proportion of A level students specialising in mathematics and the sciences, and the adequacy of the level of achievement of those students.

10.67 I asked SCAA to investigate these concerns, and the Authority created a consultation group of subject experts to help them evaluate the causes of present problems and suggest possible remedies. The recommendations in this Section of the Report reflect its advice, that of SCAA, and wider consultation.

10.68 The proportion of A level students specialising in mathematics and the sciences has declined in recent years, from 30 per cent in 1984 to 17 per cent in 1995.

10.69 There are several possible causes for this decline. Some commentators have argued that society undervalues science in terms of the rewards given to those pursuing a career in it. There is a common view that the subjects are dull or difficult. Recent research gives support to the view that mathematics and science subjects are more difficult than many other A level subjects. (See Section 10.11–10.21 on comparability between A level subjects.) An NFER[5] study in schools found that for students studying exclusively mathematics and science A levels, difficulties with mathematics were highlighted as a cause of non-completion.

10.70 In addition to the decline in numbers, there are serious concerns on the part of those in higher education and to a lesser extent amongst employers about the current requirements in A level mathematics. For example, a recent Engineering Council report[6] concluded that the engineering-related mathematical knowledge of first year undergraduate engineers is weaker now than ten years ago. The London Mathematical Society[7] has questioned whether the A level standards currently required are appropriate. My Interim Report of July 1995 referred to the concerns expressed by university vice-chancellors and to the possibility, in their view, of needing to move to a four year degree course.

10.71 In consultation over changes in the content of A level mathematics, particular reference was made to the need for more algebra in A levels. Concerns were also expressed about limited perceptions of the role of precision and proof, a declining ability to handle multi-step problems, and a lack of facility in handling number without the assistance of a calculator. These concerns about A level mathematics were shared by those teaching engineering, physics and chemistry in higher education.

10.72 We thus have a problem that, in relation to the GCSE, the requirements in mathematics and science A levels appear to be more demanding than in other subjects, and yet the adequacy of the A levels in these subjects as a preparation for university courses, especially in mathematics, is in doubt.

---

5 *The Take-up of Advanced Mathematics Courses: a Research Study*, NFER 1996, (forthcoming). *The Take-Up of Advanced Science Courses: a Research Study*, NFER 1996, (forthcoming).

6 The *Changing Mathematical Background of Undergraduate Engineers*, The Engineering Council, 1995.

7 *Tackling the Mathematics Problem*, London Mathematical Society et al, 1995.

Mathematics: The gap between the GCSE and A level

10.73 One of the constant themes to emerge from consultation and research into young people's perceptions (see Appendix B4) was the perceived gap between GCSE and A level.

10.74 As noted in Section 10.13, the step from GCSE to A level appears to be bigger in mathematics and science than in many other subjects. In mathematics, for example, to have at least a 50 per cent probability of getting a grade D or better at A level, candidates need a grade B at GCSE in mathematics, but only a grade C at GCSE in English. There is a big step between the algebra required for GCSE mathematics and the algebra required for A level mathematics and physics. In mathematics and science GCSEs, it is sometimes possible for candidates to obtain high grades without demonstrating competence in some aspects of the syllabus which are important for A level study. This possibility occurs particularly for candidates who get grade B through the 'intermediate tier' of mathematics GCSE papers, which students of middle ability generally take.

10.75 In future the top tier in the new GCSE mathematics examinations will include assessment of the extension material (ie material that goes beyond the standard provision for all students) in the National Curriculum. With A levels in mind, further challenges for potential A level candidates in mathematics, sciences and other quantitative subjects could be provided by creating a full-course, or short-course, optional GCSE in Additional Mathematics. To that end consideration should be given to constructing a single-tier, limited-grade (A*–C) examination based on existing certificates in mathematics, which do not have Section 5 approval under the Education Reform Act. The relationship of such an examination to a reformulated AS (see Section 11) would also need to be clarified.

10.76 The proposed reformulated AS, however, should encourage those who do not wish to commit themselves to a full A level in mathematics, to continue with the subject post-16, and enable more students to consider mathematics as part of their A level portfolio.

10.77 I recommend that:

■ Schools and colleges should encourage students proposing to take A level mathematics to take a GCSE paper in additional mathematics, whether equivalent in weight to a GCSE short course or a full GCSE.

■ The regulatory bodies should encourage awarding bodies to seek approval under Section 5 of the Education Act 1988, so that the existing certificates in mathematics can form a new, challenging GCSE course in additional mathematics, limited to grades A*–C.

■ The regulatory bodies should review the range of curriculum material available to support courses to bridge the gap between GCSE and A level and, if necessary, stimulate the development of additional materials.

A level mathematics

10.78 A level mathematics has to serve a number of different purposes. Some students will go on to use mathematics as a significant part of a higher education course such as mathematics, physics and engineering. At one time many of these students would have taken a second A level in further mathematics, in addition to the normal mathematics course. The number doing so has fallen from 5600 in 1990 to 4100 in 1995. Others, for example biologists, geographers and economists, will use mathematics in more of a support role in their university course. Finally, there are those who are taking mathematics simply for its own sake, and who intend to follow courses that do not require any mathematics or to go straight into employment. These groups have different requirements in terms of both the content and level of the mathematics needed. It is difficult for a single course of study to fulfil all these needs.

10.79 There are two ways in which these different needs might be met. First, courses could be differentiated by content. The mathematics studied could vary according to the purpose to which the student intends to put it. The extent to which schools and colleges could resource a number of different courses does, however, limit the scope for this approach. Moreover, the benefits need to be weighed against the need to reduce the numbers of syllabuses and options. There are at present 32 traditional and 67 modular syllabuses. Further, the concerns expressed by the universities about the coverage of mathematics syllabuses point to a need for the regulatory and awarding bodies to re-examine the content and size of the mandatory core content which applies to all syllabuses.

10.80 A second approach would be to differentiate A level examination papers by level. Introducing examination papers addressing only part of the grade range would allow the examination to focus more narrowly on material at a particular level of difficulty. As in the first approach, there could also be an element of differentiation by content.

10.81 Another approach would be to encourage schools and colleges to make more use of further mathematics, ie a paper additional to the main A level paper, as they often did in the past.

10.82 Taking into account these points, and the concerns expressed by universities and others about A level mathematics, I **recommend** that:

- The regulatory bodies, noting the concerns expressed in consultation about inadequate coverage of important areas of mathematics (see Section 10.71), drawing on the advice of the consultation group established by SCAA and the results obtained in due course from the study of standards over time, should enter into discussion with the awarding bodies about the requirements for A level mathematics including the size of the mandatory core.

- Schools and colleges should encourage students to make more use of further mathematics courses through which students can supplement the main A level course. If double mathematics is not practicable, a further mathematics course equal in weight to the AS would be of benefit.

- The regulatory bodies should enter into discussions with the awarding bodies to maintain a good range of options while reducing overlapping provision.

- The regulatory bodies should investigate the feasibility of devising A level mathematics courses targeted at specific levels of attainment, or containing content designed for specific purposes.

Science: The GCSE double award

10.83 As with mathematics, there appears to be a bigger gap between the GCSE in the physical sciences and A levels than in many other subjects.

10.84 Some evidence suggests that the GCSE double award science does not provide as good a preparation for high achievement in A levels in chemistry, physics or biology as do GCSEs in the individual sciences. Obviously double science does not provide as much time for each separate science as do the GCSEs concentrating on the individual subjects. The following tables compare A level scores in 1994 with the 1992 GCSE results of students taking double science and with those taking the individual sciences.

10.85 The interpretation of these statistics is not straightforward. Candidates with double award science also, in general, do less well in all other A level subjects. The tables should be regarded as indicative, and not as conclusive evidence.

10.86 Changes to the science curriculum with the introduction of the National Curriculum and of double award science have led to large increases in the numbers of students taking a substantial course in science for the GCSE, which is welcome. As a result we will have a much larger population literate in basic science. The emphasis given to science in the National Curriculum is one of the substantial benefits it has brought. But the broad base of general science has meant that decisions have had to be made about what is important in the science curriculum. Some material which features in the separate physics, chemistry or biology examinations has been omitted from double award science GCSEs.

10.87 There is some evidence that schools are attempting to teach double award science in less than the 20 per cent of curriculum time normally assumed to be needed, and the Royal Society, in particular, has expressed concern that less than 20 per cent is inadequate for this purpose. There is also an issue to do with the nature of the examining process at GCSE. Material that is essential for preparation for A level sciences is present in both GCSE double award and separate science syllabuses, but is not always examined thoroughly enough. Consequently some of the more demanding material, though present in syllabuses, may not be taught because it is not examined. One approach would be to develop further the existing descriptions for the award of high grades, to ensure that those achieving these grades have demonstrated the knowledge, understanding and skill required for moving on to A level study.

Table 9 Physics

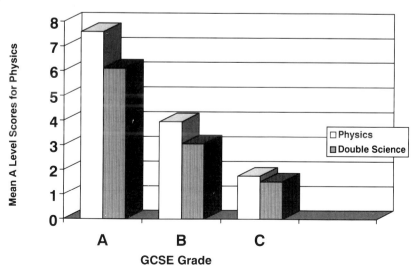

Table 10 Chemistry

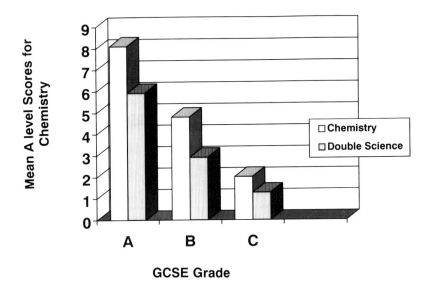

Table 11 Biology

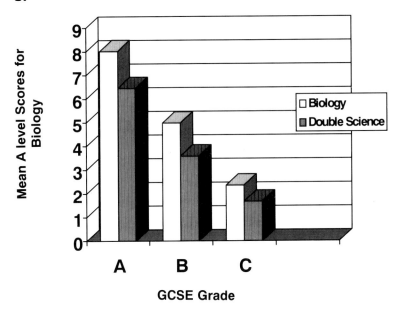

10.88 The argument that a broad science education up to the age of 16 is important for all students must be balanced against concerns that double award science does not provide as good a foundation for A level work in the individual sciences as do the corresponding GCSEs in the three separate sciences. Through their monitoring programmes the regulatory bodies need to establish whether the range of courses currently offered is sufficient to meet both concerns.

10.89 I recommend that:

■ The regulatory bodies should collect evidence to establish whether the current range of GCSE courses in the sciences satisfactorily provides both broad science education and sufficient preparation for further study at A level, and report their conclusions to the Secretaries of State.

■ Schools should use 20 per cent of curriculum time for double science, as urged by the Royal Society.

A level science

10.90 Universities receiving undergraduates to read the sciences will be helped by measures to raise levels of preparedness in mathematics as outlined above. But they would be further helped if the students coming forward to study a particular science had covered much the same ground in their A levels. At present, with a range of syllabus options at A level, the universities cannot expect all entrants to be similarly prepared, and teaching has to start at a level that will reasonably accommodate all.

10.91 On the other hand schools welcome a choice of syllabus, and diversity can enhance the quality of teaching: some teachers see one approach as suitable, challenging and interesting; others see advantages in another. A range of choice increases the chances of attracting students to take up science.

10.92 A range of syllabuses is therefore valuable. But this needs to be balanced against the university interest in having a larger common content and the need for the regulatory bodies to discharge their responsibilities of maintaining parity of standards with a reasonable level of resources. The present provision of syllabuses is as follows:

Table 12 Number of A level syllabuses[8]

	Traditional linear syllabuses	Modular syllabuses
General science	2	9
Biology	11	13
Chemistry	9	13
Physics	7	12

10.93 A reconciliation between these conflicting needs can be achieved by some increase in the size of the core, which the regulatory bodies prescribe as common content for all A levels in a subject, and by some reduction in the number of syllabus options.

10.94 Beyond these general points, I have not covered the A level content of the individual science, although I did hear concerns about the need for more inorganic chemistry. These are issues that would be pursued by SCAA through its advisory committee.

10.95 **I recommend** that:

- The regulatory bodies should enter into discussions with the awarding bodies with a view to increasing the size of the A level subject core in the sciences and reducing the number of syllabuses currently available, while maintaining some scope for a range of syllabuses.

- Awarding bodies should note the comments that some of the more demanding content of syllabuses does not feature sufficiently in examinations (see Section 10.87).

- SCAA should assess the provision for chemistry in the light of the outcome of the OFSTED/SCAA study of standards over time.

---

8   Figures exclude numbers of syllabuses in psychology, electronics, geology and science in the environment.

Improving the take-up of mathematics and the sciences at A level

10.96 A significant cause of the low take-up of mathematics and the sciences is society's attitude towards these subjects. A change in social attitudes is not achieved easily; it needs a long-term, large-scale commitment from all concerned. Nevertheless, steps can be taken to address the problem. Relevant bodies - the regulatory bodies, the inspectorates, the Teacher Training Agency, and Government Departments - should take every opportunity, through conferences, publications and contacts with the media, to promote the image of the sciences and mathematics. Local initiatives and support, such as those provided by the Science and Technology Regional Organisations and Neighbourhood Engineers, should be publicised more widely. At a more specific level, school organisational strategies (such as grouping students in sets) that have proved to be successful in encouraging students to opt for mathematics and the sciences at A level, should be disseminated. Even more important is to provide training to develop new and stimulating approaches to teaching the sciences and mathematics. The use of teaching packages which draw on communications and information technology also have a potentially valuable role here to supplement teaching, as the universities are finding. These enable students, under guidance, to follow interactive programmes through TV monitors and keyboards. Such initiatives need careful evaluation, and in the light of that, development and adoption by schools and colleges as funding becomes available.

10.97 The qualifications of teachers have a bearing on their students' achievement. The latest available data show that chemistry and physics have among the highest proportions of qualified teachers for any A level subject. In chemistry 76 per cent, and in physics 67 per cent of A level teachers have a degree in the subject. In mathematics, 63 per cent of A level teachers are mathematics graduates, but in GCSE mathematics the proportion is only 39 per cent. In that might lie part of the problem.

10.98 The influence of the quality of teaching on standards of achievement is a particularly important factor. It also bears directly on the number choosing to study a subject. Good teachers attract students. There is a lot of good practice: it provides the basis for enhancing quality across the profession through teacher training. An improvement in standards in mathematics needs to be sought long before students are approaching GCSE. It needs to be sought in the later years in primary school and right through secondary education. The OFSTED review of mathematics inspection findings[9] in 1993/94 concluded that pupils were achieving less than they were capable of in about a third of primary schools and a fifth of secondary schools.

10.99 I **recommend** that:

■ Building upon the work of the Teacher Training Agency (TTA), the regulatory bodies should develop a programme of further research into factors affecting the attitudes of parents, pupils and teachers to mathematics and the sciences, and disseminate the findings through a programme of regional conferences, newsletters and other publications for schools.

■ The regulatory bodies and the TTA should identify and disseminate measures arising from this research to encourage a greater take-up of mathematics and the sciences.

---

9   *Mathematics: A review of inspection findings 1993/94,* OFSTED.

■ Interactive learning packages of high quality designed for use in schools and colleges merit the kind of development that has been taking place in universities.

■ SCAA's mathematics and science consultative group should explore further the issues considered in this Section of the Report, with a view to some early decisions and action, and guide SCAA in further research and policy development. ACAC and CCEA should consider parallel action in Wales and Northern Ireland respectively.

The GNVQ in science

10.100 A relatively new development has been the introduction of the Science GNVQs at Intermediate and Advanced levels, available for three years now. The take-up of the Advanced Science GNVQ is currently just over 6,000 students. Between 1500 and 2000 students are expected to complete the Advanced GNVQ in July 1996. On the basis of data gathered on previous cohorts, two-thirds of students on Advanced courses will seek to enter higher education to study science.

10.101 Just over 4000 students are aiming for the Intermediate Science GNVQ. These students would have previously studied a BTEC First certificate in Science or the GCSE. Most of these students aim to continue their study of science.

10.102 Research by the NCVQ indicates that the Intermediate and Advanced Science GNVQ students are new to post-16 science. In response to a questionnaire survey, the Advanced GNVQ students stated that they would not have taken A level sciences. The emphasis in the GNVQ on the practical application of science is a distinctive approach which seems to be attracting a wider cohort of students. Employers value the way the GNVQs encourage students to develop a wide range of general skills such as the ability to work well in teams and communication skills. Higher education tutors are also recognising the advantage that students with these skills have. Research commissioned for the Review into the expectations of employers and higher education of 16–19 year olds taking Advanced level qualifications in science is relevant in this context (see Appendix B6).

10.103 If students with GNVQs are successful in their higher education courses and employers find them to be effective in their work, more students may be encouraged to study science through this route.

10.104 I **recommend** that:

■ The NCVQ should continue to consult with universities and employers to monitor the progress of the science GNVQ closely, so that its quality and fitness for purpose are assured, with a view to the GNVQ at Advanced level providing an additional source of scientists and science technicians.

SECTION 11

A reformulated AS

11.1 The Advanced Supplementary (AS) was introduced in 1987 as a way of encouraging students to broaden their A level studies. But take-up has remained low. Figures for 1995 showed a decline in entries, to fewer than 50,000 for the whole of England, Wales and Northern Ireland. For every fifteen A levels, only one AS is taken. A recent report by the Office for Standards in Education (OFSTED)[1] noted that though AS courses in at least one subject were taught in approximately 60 per cent of schools, few offered more than two subjects. A major problem has been the difficulties of timetabling the AS; most schools cannot afford to run separate A level and AS courses.

11.2 The Further Education Development Agency (FEDA) has drawn attention to the fact that the AS represents a sizeable part of the subject core of the A level in many subjects. The core can be intellectually demanding, and may be particularly abstract and theoretical in some subjects. For the AS to be devoted to the most intellectually demanding content of the full A level is to make it relatively more demanding than the A level itself. This is not the most appropriate choice of content for the first year of an A level course, nor the best transition from the GCSE for most learners. This observation has particular significance in the light of the widespread view of students, teachers and others that the 'gap' between the current GCSE and A level study is a problem for many learners. 85 per cent of A level students in a survey of young people's perceptions carried out for this Review (see Appendix B4) considered there was a big jump in demand between GCSEs and their post-16 courses.

11.3 The Interim Report also cited evidence from consultations by the Schoool Curriculum and Assessment Authority (SCAA) that the current 'vertical' AS, designed to be half the content of the full A level but at the same standard, was not working. The low take-up, and the evident failure of the present AS to achieve its purpose of encouraging breadth in post-16 education, points to the need for a reformulation.

Consultation

11.4 Consultation during Stage Two of the Review has confirmed the initial support for a reformulated AS from most of the major bodies representing schools and colleges. Almost all the GCE awarding bodies, including the Council for the Curriculum, Examinations and Assessment (CCEA) in Northern Ireland, where the current AS has had the lowest take-up, have confirmed their support. Many individual respondents have also welcomed the proposal in the Interim Report that a reformulation of the present AS should be explored, in particular as a means of promoting greater breadth in the 16–19 study programmes of more students.

11.5 There is, however, a significant minority which argues against the introduction of a new 'Intermediate' qualification, between GCSE and A level, as an unnecessary and unhelpful addition to an already complex framework.

---

[1] *Effective Sixth Forms*, OFSTED, 1996

11.6 In its response, the Confederation of British Industry (CBI) questioned whether the case for a reformulated AS had been proven, and cautioned that 'it is not clear that a horizontal AS would be valued by employers.' However, they agreed that it is right to search for ways of encouraging academic students to take more than two or three subjects. In subsequent discussions they recognised that the continued low take-up of the present AS made a case for a new approach.

11.7 Comments at consultation conferences, particularly from the further education sector, often indicated a preference for an AS as part of a national system of credit accumulation and transfer rather than as a separate qualification.

11.8 The Association of University Teachers, while expressing reservations about the AS (current or reformulated), also acknowledged that: 'The strongest justification for an intermediate stage of some description in the 16–19 period is that the staying on rate falls dramatically after a year, and students who drop out have little or nothing to show for a year's work. Moreover if they want to re-enter post-compulsory education at a later stage they have nothing tangible to build upon.'

11.9 Overall, there was wide support for the objectives which a reformulated AS sought to meet: to provide a qualification which is economic to teach, which reduces wastage and encourages breadth of study. A reformulated AS could thus provide either a staging-post on the way to a full A level, or a worthwhile award for students who choose to go no further.

11.10 The crucial point is that the present AS has not succeeded in its objective of promoting greater breadth in A level study in the eight years of its existence. There is wide agreement that we do need to encourage more students to broaden their studies, and a new approach is therefore needed. This proposal will make it easier to accommodate the AS within the main timetable of A level work. It should be more attractive to students and would be more convincing as an award which truly represents half the workload of a full A level.

Principles for reformulating the AS

11.11 The Interim Report suggested that the current AS might be reformulated, 'so that instead of covering half an A level syllabus in depth, it would cover the syllabus content in the breadth and depth appropriate for one year's study post-GCSE.' (Interim Report Section 14.11.)

11.12 This working definition has been the basis for consultation during Stage Two of the Review.

11.13 Five possible groups of learners have been identified for a reformulated AS.

- Those who wish to broaden their post-16 course (the primary purpose).

- Those who, initially at least, are prepared to commit themselves only to one more year in full-time education.

- Those who are not yet sure about the areas in which they wish to specialise and who would like to defer their decision until later.

- Those learners considered not yet able, mature or confident enough to cope with a full A level course, and those who have chosen to take only a short course in the GCSE and for whom therefore the AS would represent a substantial advance.

- Adults returning to study (full or part-time) for whom a full A level may, at first, seem a difficult and distant goal.

11.14 In consultation, three principles were suggested for a reformulated AS.

- **Coherence.** The AS must have its own internal coherence and not be seen simply as a step to another qualification. But it must also be designed for progression, and its place within the 16–19 qualifications framework should be clearly understood.

- **Common Teaching.** If schools and colleges are to be able to offer a wide range of AS courses, these must be capable of being taught alongside the full A level. In most situations this means common teaching programmes. Within a modular scheme (for example, a six-module A level), the first three modules would constitute the reformulated AS.

- **Currency.** It should have a currency in its own right, as well as being recognised as a key contributor to the objective of encouraging greater breadth in the programmes of 16–19 year olds.

11.15 This is a demanding set of requirements, but if a new approach is to succeed, it must respond to them.

11.16 To help inform thinking on this issue, and recognising that different subjects may need to be treated differently, five subject advisory groups were commissioned during Stage Two of the Review to consider a possible model for a reformulated AS. Participants were invited to contribute as specialists in their subject areas. Their views are given in Appendix G5. Their overall conclusion was that the full A level should build up from the AS, not vice-versa. As one headteacher put it, the AS should be 'geared to breadth as a principle, rather than constructed as a watered down or shortened version of existing A level programmes'.

The standard and level of a reformulated AS

11.17 Many respondents to consultation have argued that the standard of the new AS should be 'half way between GCSE and A level'. Some have argued that the AS should accredit achievement which ranges, after one year's Advanced level study, from the top end of GCSE up to the full A level standard.

11.18 The need for a spread of grades to reflect different levels of achievement raises the issue of 'maturation'. Currently, both the AS and A levels, as well as the Advanced GNVQ, require all modules and units to be of the same standard, irrespective of when they are taken. In A levels, different levels of achievement in the modules are reflected in grades. In the GNVQ, the comparable units are not graded. The requirement for all A level modules to be at the same standard has been challenged particularly in skills-based subjects like modern foreign languages and music, where common sense suggests that students' performance at the end of a two-year course will be better than after, say, six months or a year.

11.19 Some allowance should therefore be made for maturation to help bridge the gap between GCSE and Advanced level. This implies a need to consider a lower weighting for units or modules taken early in a course when these count towards a full A level within a modular scheme of assessment. Careful consideration will need to be given to the relative weighting of the AS grade when it contributes to the full A level. It will be essential to ensure that the overall A level standard is safeguarded whilst, at the same time, making due allowance for maturation during the A level course.

11.20 The issue for the reformulated AS is what achievement might reasonably be expected half-way through the full A level course, and whether this needs a new name and designation within the overall framework of qualifications.

11.21 In the context of this Review, which seeks to increase the coherence and intelligibility of the current framework, the formal creation of a new additional level between the GCSE and A levels could prove counter-productive. A reformulated AS which bridges GCSE and A levels, referenced against these benchmarks, and with explicit linkages to both, has attractions. But it may be unduly confusing to students, their parents and other users of the qualification. I therefore propose below a solution which avoids undue complexity, relates to current practice in many schools and colleges when assessing students through internal examinations, and reflects the experience of other examination systems which offer main and subsidiary qualifications side by side.

11.22 Having examined the case for a reformulated AS and its possible form, I **recommend** that:

- A new AS should be developed as a means of encouraging greater breadth of study in full-time 16–19 education and training and to reduce wastage for students who do not proceed to the full A level. Those intending to take the full A level should, if they wished, be able to progress to it without taking the AS.

- The new AS should be graded on an A–E scale like the full A level, with the top grade defined as the standard attained by a student who, with one year's further study, would be expected to achieve grade A in the full A level; the other grades would relate to the A level standard in the same way. Although this approach may appear to lack precision, it is the basis on which students are regularly assessed in many schools and colleges at the end of their first year's post-16 study. Grades would be indicative and informative to students, parents, teachers and higher education in the case of those intending to continue to the full A level. For those who go no further, the grades would attest to a level of achievement comparable to that of a full A level but in relation to half the content at a subsidiary level.

- The content of the new AS should be the equivalent of half a full A level course (designed to occupy half the teaching time of a typical two-year advanced level course, or three modules out of six in a modular scheme).

- The new AS should count as half an A level in terms of performance tables and the proposed new UCAS tariff, and the National Targets for Education and Training.

- The new AS should be re-named as **Advanced Subsidiary** (AS). Although there would be merit in moving away from the acronym of the current, unsuccessful AS, 'Advanced Subsidiary' is the most accurate description of its place within the qualifications framework and its relationship with the full A level. It is, moreover, already familiar as an acronym, if not widely understood. It would be easier to build on this than start from scratch. Serious consideration should, however, be given to the marketing of the new AS to students, parents, teachers, employers and higher education. Considerable planning and careful thought will be needed to ensure successful promotion of a subsidiary qualification of this sort, and what it could add, particularly in the context of breadth.

■ The current A and AS level subject cores should be reviewed and, where necessary, revised to position the new AS core as the 'foundation', with additional A level content expressed as 'extension' material. Subject cores would need to take account of the proposed redistribution of content between AS and A level to ensure that the new AS:

☐ builds on and extends both the content and level of demand of the GCSE syllabus (full or short course);

☐ focuses on those aspects of the current A level which are most relevant to young people who want to go beyond GCSE but who may not want to progress to the full A level;

☐ also provides directly for progression to other qualifications within the framework, in particular A levels, but also in appropriate subjects, the Advanced GNVQ.

■ In such subjects, the first module or unit of the new AS should be based on common content drawn from the full A level/GNVQ. The next two modules/units could be designed as 'transitional' units to give learners a proper feel for the content and approach of the parent qualification (A level or GNVQ) and prepare them for the second half of the course.

■ Further consideration should also be given by NCVQ to the development of a new 'Applied AS' based on three unit groupings from the full GNVQ. (See Section 9.16.)

■ The regulatory bodies should examine the case for a new AS in a small number of subjects which are currently not available, but which might make a particular contribution to 'breadth' (for example, economic and industrial understanding, environmental education, European awareness, and citizenship).

■ A new, free-standing, single AS should be developed in 'key skills' (communication, the application of number and information technology) as proposed in Section 7.29-7.32.

■ The current AS should be phased out as soon as the new AS can be introduced, since to retain it would only add to confusion and complexity.

■ The regulatory bodies should undertake a pilot study immediately to assess the implications for different subjects of a reformulated AS, including the timetabling and likely resource issues for schools and colleges of offering such courses. The study should pay particular attention to: subject differences; flexible patterns for delivering the AS; the scope for common teaching of the AS with the full A level; and whether students proceeding to the full A level should bypass the AS in order to reduce the burden of external assessment and additional examination entry fees.

SECTION 12

Recognising a wider range of achievement

12.1   All students have their own individual needs. But the four groups discussed in this Section stand out as needing particular thought. These are:

Lower attainers   Those who, though not having a statement of special educational needs, nevertheless have real difficulty in learning and typically do not attain grade G at GCSE or its vocational equivalent.

Under-achievers   Those who have the potential to do considerably better but from the age of 14 or earlier reject the conventional academic curriculum offered to them, and often achieve little during compulsory school years.

Those with learning difficulties   Those with major learning difficulties who are likely to have had a statement of Special Educational Needs (SEN) at school.

Those with exceptional ability   The ablest few in whatever pathway they have chosen.

12.2   Such groupings are not intended to suggest that solutions need to be discrete, but rather to focus on particular needs. The most important principle in addressing the needs of these learners must be that we should aim to provide appropriate stimulation and challenges to all learners.

The recognition of achievement by lower attainers

12.3   Lower attainers are those at the age of 14 and beyond who are not succeeding at school and who are not likely to achieve even a GCSE grade G. Grade G approximates to the achievement of the average 11 year old. Although my proposals are also relevant to those with learning difficulties (see Sections 12.40–12.51), my particular concern here is with those young people who are at the lower end of the normal ability range, having perhaps in their early years made poor progress in reading and consequently struggled throughout their school careers, but who still have the potential to better their current achievements.

The scale of the problem

12.4   The following table shows the percentage not achieving GCSE passes in English, mathematics, or in any other GCSE, and indicates the scale of the problem.

Table 13

Year	Number of Year 11 pupils	% not entered for any GCSE	% not achieving any GCSE Passes (A*–G)	% not achieving a GCSE Pass in English	% not achieving a GCSE Pass in Maths	% not achieving a GCSE Pass in English and Maths	% not achieving a GCSE Pass in English, Maths and Science
1994	532,000	6	8	15	17	19	21
1993	522,000	6	7	12	20	21	23
1992	544,000	7	8	13	21	23	25

12.5 Overall, the data suggest that with the exception of English, the proportion of students for whom GCSE is 'not appropriate' is falling. Nevertheless, the number of students for whom GCSE appears to be out of immediate reach remains large. Just over 40,000 do not achieve any GCSE passes at all. Nearly 80,000 fail to achieve a pass in English; over 90,000 in mathematics, and over 100,000 in English and mathematics together. It is a matter for national concern that nearly one in five of the cohort does not achieve even a grade G in both English and mathematics.

12.6 These statistics are complemented by:

■ Keele University figures indicating that 20 per cent of students in their last year of statutory schooling played truant, and that 25 per cent of secondary pupils sometimes or often behave badly.[1]

■ A recent survey by the Basic Skills Agency which showed that around 15 per cent of a representative sample of 21 year olds had significant difficulties with basic literacy and numeracy.[2]

12.7 Another aspect of the problem is the achievement gap at 16 between the sexes. Girls out-perform boys in almost all subject areas, including science, at GCSE. The following table demonstrates that in English and mathematics the problem of low achievement is particularly marked amongst boys. This issue is addressed further in Section 14.

Table 14 Percentage not getting a GCSE Pass in 1994

	English %	Mathematics %	Both subjects %
Boys	17	19	21
Girls	12	15	16

1   *Young People and their Attitudes to School:* Keele University August 1994 – Professor Michael Barber.

2   *Difficulties with Basic Skills: Findings from the 1970 British Cohort Study* A summary, Basic Skills Agency, September 1995, John Bynner and Jane Steedman.

12.8 It is also sometimes said that lower attainers largely identify themselves by the end of Key Stage 1, at age 7, by low performance in literacy and number. Once children have fallen behind, the gap between them and their contemporaries tends to get ever wider. This is at least partially true. The Basic Skills Agency found that 'at age 10, there is a quite a high degree of predictability about basic skills difficulty in adulthood.'

12.9 These statistics indicate that there is a problem. And while the reform of the National Curriculum should help to reduce the numbers of lower attainers in the future, there will still be those who need a little longer time to get on to the existing qualifications ladder.

12.10 Those who can achieve through the GCSE, GNVQ or NVQ are covered by the National Awards proposed in Section 3 of this Report. For the others there is no system of nationally recognised awards.

12.11 The creation of a GCSE grade (or grades) below G is not the answer. The GCSE already covers a very wide range of achievement, and to stretch it further by creating a grade H would be going too far.

12.12 Various awarding bodies and local authorities have developed qualifications to meet the need, and in Wales such a qualification has been introduced nationally – the Certificate of Education (CoE). But these awards do not have wider currency across England and Wales. A national award would give these students recognition with wide national currency, which is a significant consideration in today's geographically mobile society.

12.13 On the other hand it has generally been considered in consultation to be undesirable and impractical to introduce a single qualification for this group, with its diverse needs. The client group encompasses all ages, a very mixed ability range (which includes those with a wide range of special needs), and a range of contexts extending from school to training and evening classes. A single qualification would lack the flexibility needed to serve so diverse a population. It would, moreover, take years to establish itself and undermine the work of those who have created the present qualifications. Their continued commitment is very much needed.

12.14 The alternative approach is to lift the standing of the present qualifications by specifying common standards, introducing visible, consistent quality assurance into this area, and granting to qualifications that meet these standards recognition at the Entry level in the wider national qualifications framework. This line of development would be wholly consistent with that which has underpinned the design of the Certificate of Educational Achievement, which is to replace the Welsh CoE in 1997. Such recognition would indicate to all that the achievements of these young people are at a nationally recognised standard. The approach favoured during consultation would give priority to devising such standards in communication, the application of number and information technology. The sources for the standards would be the National Curriculum level descriptions, contextualised for the age group, GCSE grade descriptions, the NCVQ units in these skills at Foundation level and the Basic Skills Agency's expertise. Qualifications would then be devised or adapted to these standards, which would offer clear routes of progression into both relevant GCSEs and NCVQ units, in the three key skills.

12.15 I **recommend** that priority should be given to approving existing awards that develop key skills at Entry level; over time, the provision should become much wider than these to encompass the many valuable programmes which are offered at this level and which should be eligible for formal recognition at this level.

12.16 I **recommend** this approach, and propose that the key criteria for approving or kitemarking awards at Entry level should be the following:

■ The units of award should be clearly specified in terms of learning outcomes which describe in a clear language what the learner is expected to know, understand and do as a result of achieving the unit.

■ The award should be designed to provide opportunities for progression to higher levels.

■ The awarding body should have adequate internal quality assurance mechanisms for its processes.

■ The awarding body should have a commitment to equal access.

12.17 Awards meeting these standards would come into the National Framework of Qualifications, be known as the Entry level, and carry the Entry level headings. The face of the award, as part of the national family, would be as illustrated in Appendix C5 and at the end of Section 3 of this Report. Qualifications at Entry level would be available though the revised Youth Training (see Section 5) as well as through school and college-based provision.

12.18 SCAA and ACAC, using the powers of Section 5[3] of the Education Reform Act 1988, have already made the first systematic attempt to ensure that non-GCSE qualifications offered pre-16 in schools conform to some basic quality standards, including links with the National Curriculum and appropriate progression opportunities. These powers have proved to be a useful means to the end of providing high quality options for accreditation for these young people. Although such measures have not hitherto been thought to be necessary post-16, there are latent powers in Section 24 of the Education Reform Act to apply these arrangements to qualifications offered to 16–18 year olds in full-time education. The need for greater coherence, concerns about proliferation of syllabuses, and the desire to enhance quality assurance (not just for Entry level qualifications, but more widely) now argue for a reconsideration of this. Consideration should therefore be given to implementing the powers in Section 24 of the Education Reform Act to achieve these objectives and to tackle the wider problems of comparability which are considered in Section 10.

Implementation

12.19 Encouragement for the take-up of these nationally approved Entry level qualifications might involve:

---

[3] This provides that 'no course of study leading to a qualification authenticated by an outside person shall be provided for pupils of compulsory school age by or an behalf of any maintained school unless the qualification is approved by the Secretaries of State or by a designated body'. Circulars are issued annually by the DfEE and the Welsh Office providing guidance on qualifications and syllabuses that have been approved for use by pupils of compulsory school age in maintained schools (including grant-maintained special schools) in England and Wales. The qualifications are approved by the Secretaries of State, and the syllabuses by SCAA and ACAC.

■ Publicity for the standards.

■ Guidance for schools, colleges and training providers.

■ Removing, after due notice, qualifications that aim at this market and do not conform to the standards from the Section 5 list, and not approving them under Section 24 of the Education Reform Act, if implemented.

■ Ensuring that only nationally recognised qualifications form part of the proposed National Entry level provision (see Section 5 of the Report).

12.20 If this approach is agreed, the next steps would be to:

■ Confirm the standards, building on work already started by the regulatory bodies under Section 5 of the 1988 Education Reform Act, for qualifications below grade G of GCSE.

■ Invite awarding bodies to revise their qualifications against the standards (see Appendix H1).

■ Check awarding bodies and qualifications against the standards.

■ Introduce the National Award as illustrated in Appendix C5.

■ Issue guidance and publicity materials.

12.21 Thereafter there would be a need to ensure that standards are maintained.

12.22 This approach would bring coherence to the present range of individual awards, help to raise standards, send a signal that qualifications in this area are valued nationally, and provide clear access to the next steps in the national qualifications framework.

12.23 I **recommend** that:

■ Any award below grade G in GCSE and the Foundation level of the GNVQ that meets the national standards prescribed by the regulatory bodies, should qualify for a certificate confirming that it is a National Award at Entry level.

■ To be recognised as a National Award at Entry level, an award should be designed to offer progression to Foundation level.

■ In accrediting such national awards, priority should be given in the short term to awards in communication, the application of number and information technology. Competence in information technology is often a good motivator and will increasingly become a fundamental element in working life.

■ In order to facilitate this accreditation, consideration should be given to implementing the powers in Section 24 of the Education Reform Act.

Under-achievers: A response through new opportunities at age 14

12.24 Under-achievers may be of any ability. They characteristically have the potential to achieve considerably more, but fall behind for a variety of reasons, such as disaffection, truancy, severe difficulties at home, or personal psychological problems.

12.25 The prospects for such young people in the next century are poor. Educational attainment will be increasingly a pre-condition of employment. Under-achievers who cannot find or keep jobs may become disaffected citizens. In turn, there is a risk that they will pass their attitudes to their children. The children of parents with low standards of literacy tend to find themselves at a disadvantage at school.

12.26 As children become adolescents, they are increasingly likely to distance themselves from failure by opting-out. They are likely to fail to see the relevance of the traditional curriculum taught in schools, with its long-term goals and academic focus. The more this happens, the wider the gap between them and the rest of the class is likely to become. To protect their own self-esteem, such pupils may reject school altogether and adopt other values, possibly in association with others, forming an anti-culture. They may become aggressive and highly dysfunctional in class. Such pupils become more likely to be excluded from school and may end up in an educational limbo, relying on a few hours a week of home tuition or part-time attendance at a Pupil Referral Unit.

12.27 By using different curriculum delivery methods and approaches, outstanding teachers can of course make a real difference, particularly for younger children. But the problem requires a different approach from support work within the standard academic curriculum.

12.28 The consultation underpinning this Review suggests that the essence of a successful response involves setting alight some interest. Initially it hardly matters what the subject area is. Once interest has been captured, there is a basis for re-establishing relations with the student. Further education colleges have a long history of catering for learners who have been unsuccessful in school, and have developed considerable expertise in making provision which enables learners who have 'delayed' their education to re-enter the system at a later date. This is often accomplished by motivating learners through a new, more vocationally relevant activity. From this it may be possible to address the key skills of communication and the application of number. Since lack of progress in these skills has often symbolised failure at school, they are often not addressed head on, but introduced on the back of other studies which are motivating to the learner.

12.29 Learning from experience in further education, the most obvious alternative to the traditional curriculum for 14–16 year olds is the world of applied knowledge, taken forward in a school context, but also involving experience of a working environment to give meaning to the school-based work.

12.30 Young people who have rejected school are more likely to see the world of work as relating to the adult world, and therefore giving a basis for value and self-esteem. It is essential for any such alternative to be presented as a meaningful opportunity reflecting the student's own interests, and not as a response to failure.

12.31 The Foundation level GNVQs and NVQs give clear opportunities. A full GNVQ or NVQ is very large indeed as a qualification for a student who has fallen behind, but they are structured in units, each of which is a recognised achievement. This is particularly important for young people who find it difficult to look beyond the short term.

12.32 Taking advantage of this, one approach would be to introduce units of GNVQs and NVQs to make coherent learning programmes in areas which are of interest to the student, and in which there is a significant local presence of industry and commerce, so that the learning is meaningful and there is a prospect of some work experience. Following the Technical and Vocational Education Initiative (TVEI), many schools are already beginning to introduce GNVQ units for 14–16 year olds. And some schools are piloting the Part One GNVQ, equivalent in size to two GCSEs, which is available to young people of all abilities. The group work which characterises GNVQs has a further distinct advantage. It gives an opportunity to tackle negative attitudes which may have developed among the disaffected students by creating a new positive culture of achievement through working together in groups.

12.33 I **recommend** that students should have opportunities to take approved GNVQ units at Foundation and Intermediate levels from 14 onwards, as well as Entry level qualifications. For NVQs the situation is rather different. Although NVQs are provided in some schools, and most colleges, they are essentially designed for the workplace. The scope for using particular NVQ units therefore needs to be carefully addressed and whether schools and colleges can provide valid simulations of the workplace environment, and whether satisfactory assessment of NVQ competence can be arranged. At present, few NVQ units are approved for use by pupils pre-16, and I **recommend** that SCAA and ACAC should consider, together with the NCVQ, which NVQs, or NVQ units might be appropriate. These could then be approved for use in schools under Section 5 of the Education Reform Act.

12.34 Once interest in the practical side of the study has been captured through GNVQ or NVQ units, the way is open to advance in the key skills of communication and the application of number. Students are more likely to see these as relevant when they are integrated into their practical work.

12.35 Other opportunities to recapture the interest of these students are provided through extra-curricular approaches such as the Duke of Edinburgh's Award, Young Enterprise and the Youth Award Scheme accredited through the Award Scheme Development and Accreditation Network (ASDAN). These and other programmes have been found to be highly motivating, and can be taken successfully by young people across the whole ability range. The Youth Award Scheme may be taken as an example. Awards for achievement are made at four levels: they cover the age range from 14–19; they leave much scope for the development of programmes by the individual institutions; and they are designed to give the opportunity for activities that support academic study.

12.36 Integral to such schemes is the opportunity to earn an award. This is fundamental to all efforts to realise the potential in these pupils. Their greatest need is to succeed and regain some self-esteem, after what may have been years of being seen as a failure at school.

12.37 The use of information technology can also have a salutary effect on motivating and raising achievements of young people who have not previously found success in education. Integrated Learning Systems, for example, have been found in the USA to have a marked impact on achievement of key skills, and are being piloted in the UK. Teachers in this country have also commented on the motivating effect of information technology. The computer can allow young people the freedom to experiment and control the pace of their own work. It can allow them to gain in self-esteem and confidence, providing instant feedback and improving the ability to concentrate.

12.38 For some students, links with the more 'adult' environment of a local further education college may also be motivating. For a school with limited resources, this may be a practical way of opening up new learning opportunities. But such links need to be carefully structured and planned by each individual school. The increased flexibility in the revised National Curriculum from September 1996 (up to 40 per cent for some 14–16 year olds and 50 per cent in Wales) will increase the scope for such opportunities.

12.39 I **recommend** that further support should be given at national level to existing initiatives designed to provide motivation and opportunity among under-achievers where traditional education has not succeeded. While school will provide the centre for the student's continued development, education related to the adult world, with opportunities for group and project work, offers potential for those who fail to see any point or relevance to school or a traditional academic curriculum. This is especially so if a part of the student's development post-14 is in a different environment, such as a college of further education, the workplace, or simulations of it. The central objective should reflect concern to serve students well in ways that are meaningful to them, whilst maintaining the entitlement to the statutory curriculum.

Young people with learning difficulties

12.40 Many students with learning difficulties will be able to gain accreditation for their achievements through the Entry level qualifications proposed in Sections 12.14–12.23. Others will benefit from the measures described in Section 14, which deals with equal opportunities for all pupils.

12.41 Nevertheless, there are students who will need further specific provision in order to have their achievements recognised.

12.42 These students do not form a discrete group. They will be on a continuum of learning difficulties the boundaries of which are imprecise. Most may be characterised as pupils with moderate and severe learning difficulties (including pupils who have profound and multiple learning difficulties). If they are still in school, they will generally have a statement of special educational needs. Post-16, they may well go on to college, or to Youth Training, where they will be identified as having special training needs. At 14 years of age, these pupils will require a 'transition plan', under the *Code of Practice on the Identification and Assessment of Special Educational Needs,* which identifies curricular and other provision, including opportunities to gain accreditation to the age of 19 and beyond.

12.43 Although these students struggle to make progress in areas which require cognitive and quick manipulative skills, they may have other qualities that should be developed and recognised. Moreover they need to be helped and encouraged to develop skills that will equip them to live independent lives.

12.44 In that context, there is a strong case for fostering and recognising the progress they make in developing 'Skills for Adult Life' through awards at the Entry level. These might cover the following:

■ Personal skills and qualities valued in employment: for example team working skills and reliability (in terms of regularity of attendance, good time keeping, attention to detail, and steady application to tasks).

■ Family and parenting skills, for example relationships between partners, the care of children, the responsibilities of parents, what is involved in setting up a home.

■ Living independently, cooking, basic home maintenance, the care of clothes, understanding and managing money, and travelling.

■ Understanding some of the structures of the society in which they live, for example transport services, social services, the Citizens Advice Bureaux and Job Centres.

12.45 Many students in this group already spend a substantial proportion of time from the age of 14 developing these skills. Their achievements should receive recognition. These skills are not relevant only to young people with learning difficulties. Team working, regular attendance and application are among the skills most valued by employers in all employees. With the progressive loss of the extended family concentrated in one locality, interest in parenting skills has become widespread. All young people need to learn how to manage their money effectively and to become active citizens contributing to society to the best of their ability. There is a case for extending recognition of these skills more widely and opening up progression routes towards other qualifications in 'Skills for Adult Life' at higher levels in the national framework of qualifications.

12.46 A number of qualifications relating to 'life skills' already exists. Some are approved under Section 5 of the Education Reform Act. Others are at various stages of development. However, in future, before being included under Section 5, the possible new Section 24 lists, or as a part of the new National Entry level provision, qualifications in this area should comply with nationally approved criteria. They should be designed to ensure high quality and status, and become part of the National Entry level family of certificates proposed in this Report. The specified content and criteria for an award covering these life skills needs to be developed, with each of the four elements tentatively identified in Section 12.44, being individually assessed, recognised and recorded.

12.47 This is one specific proposal. In addition, there is a general need to recognise the small steps in achievement which (for many of these young people) represent substantial advances. This need includes recognition of progress in the key skills within the National Entry level of qualifications. The needs of pupils with moderate and severe learning difficulties are often highly individualised, and accreditation of their progress may not be possible through courses specified centrally. To cater for the full range of pupils, it may be necessary to develop units of work written specifically for individuals or groups which are then accredited and recognised formally. Such schemes have been developed by the Open College Networks and the Northern Partnership for Records of Achievement, which operate their own quality assurance mechanisms.

12.48 This 'unit accreditation' focuses on clearly defined elements of individual learning and accredits small steps of progress made by pupils with learning difficulties. Units are devised with specific students in mind to define the learning and the outcomes which should take place. Although such schemes are not restricted to pupils with learning difficulties, they are sufficiently flexible to pinpoint and recognise specific achievement. Achievement of accredited units or steps towards them are reported in the National Record of Achievement. (See Section 6.)

12.49 The standing of such small steps in achievement will be enhanced if they are supported by non-bureaucratic arrangements to underpin their quality.

12.50 As units are often developed to meet the needs of individual pupils, it would however be impossible to set standards against which the content of every unit could be measured. The alternative is for the awarding bodies to lay down guidelines for unit writers. But, and it needs emphasising, heavy-handed procedures are not needed. Schools and colleges should also work together to ensure that they are not spending time 'reinventing the wheel' and devising almost identical units of accreditation, rather than sharing their expertise and units.

12.51 I **recommend** that:

■ Courses to accredit skills for independent adult life should be developed against, or revised to meet, nationally recognised criteria, drawn up by the regulatory bodies with approval from the Secretaries of State. These should then be included in the Section 5 list of qualifications recognised by the Government for teaching in schools pre-16 and/or in the possible Section 24 list for provision to full-time 16–18 students. These should be at the Entry level in the proposed National Framework, but consideration should be given to the need for further qualifications in those skills at higher levels, to provide progression routes.

■ In addition the regulatory bodies should devise simple quality assurance measures for schemes to accredit small, worthwhile steps of progress by those with severe learning difficulties.

Young people of exceptional ability

12.52 While increasing attention has been devoted to the needs of young people with learning difficulties, there has been a tendency to pay less attention to outstandingly able pupils.

12.53 The especially able should not be seen in purely academic terms. Other talents (for example in the graphic arts, theatre, music, manual skills, athletic prowess) are equally deserving of attention, as are those talents which find their expression in the vocational routes.

12.54 Any response to the needs of such young people involves challenging them and recognising their achievements.

12.55 Providing them with guidance and opportunities to advance beyond their peer group in their chosen fields of learning may be the appropriate response for many. For others, there may be a greater need to encourage them to develop some breadth in knowledge and understanding, so that there is an additional dimension to their thinking. For others there may be a need to help them to develop as human beings, or to develop social or communication skills.

12.56 The liberating effect of information technology can benefit all young people. Effective use of learning resources, such as CD-ROMs, will allow more able children to access wider ranges of information, and to make connections between different areas of information, broadening and enriching their educational experience. Communications technology, such as access to the Internet, can also give them access to experts, databases and centres of excellence.

12.57 The following options are either available or suggested for consideration to respond to the needs of young people of exceptional ability. Attention is first given to options based on depth of study, and then to the possibility of development through adding breadth.

Special Papers

12.58 Special Papers (commonly known as 'S levels') provide a means of extending intellectually able students by offering them the opportunity to demonstrate and be assessed on more complex intellectual skills and to have their achievements recognised. Discussions indicate that the majority of the able young people who take Special Papers find them a rewarding experience. Many teachers also find it highly rewarding to teach these courses to small groups of able young people.

12.59 Nevertheless Special Papers have been declining rapidly in popularity. Numbers of students sitting them have fallen from 17,400 in 1989 to 9,500 in 1994. The fall has been particularly steep in mathematics, where the take-up is less than a third of its previous level. Reasons for this general decline include the following:

- Some centres are reluctant to encourage specialisation and prefer to offer 'breadth' rather than 'depth'.

- Some centres (particularly in the further education sector, where Special Papers do not carry funding units) find it difficult to provide extra tuition for small numbers of pupils in individual subjects.

- A lack of credit given to Special Papers by institutions of higher education, who see achievement as measuring the strength of the teaching institution as much as that of the pupil.

- Some feeling among universities that at this stage students might benefit more from other forms of development.

12.60 With the decline in take-up of Special Papers, one awarding body has withdrawn its provision and others are considering their position. They have therefore turned to consideration of how to maintain the Special Papers on a reasonably economic basis through sharing responsibility for provision. This would mean that Special Papers would no longer be attached to individual syllabuses as is the case at present, but rather a joint paper would exist across each subject. This may enable the awarding bodies to make Special Paper provision economic. A policy of basing a Special Paper on the standard subject core of the relevant A level could also increase the take-up by schools, since it becomes a more economic proposition from the teaching standpoint and could be taught in ordinary A level classes.

12.61 I have therefore encouraged the awarding bodies to develop a co-ordinated approach, dividing responsibility amongst themselves for the subjects covered.

12.62 Special Papers should be retained, based on common subject cores wherever possible. The awarding bodies should be encouraged to collaborate on cost-effective provision. Once the Special Paper has been reformulated, consideration should be given to recognising achievement through the proposed new UCAS tariff. In the interests of stability, a commitment should be made to provide reconstituted Special Papers for at least four years.

12.63 In the meantime, consideration should be given by the regulatory and awarding bodies, in consultation with higher education, to developing alternative approaches to the Special Papers. This might include externally marked extended assignments in which students research and explain an issue in depth. Other approaches which commanded most support or interest during consultation are considered below. Many of them provide the same level of challenge as Special Papers, and some are more readily provided by a wider range of institutions.

Taking university modules

12.64 An alternative approach is for the student of exceptional ability, by arrangement between the school or college and an institution of higher education, to take modules of a university course, and to get recognition for them on entry to the university. In some cases it may be possible to think in terms of gaining credit for the first year of a university course.

12.65 The scope for this is limited. Higher education has not developed a national system of credit accumulation and recognition, and with the diversity of higher education institutions a national system seems unlikely. There are, moreover, disadvantages to the student from being removed from close association with a peer group. Nevertheless, some students find themselves at university going over ground they have previously covered at school or college or through independent study. This is not a problem for able students only. For example, the range of syllabuses for A level students of mathematics and the sciences makes it difficult for universities to start from a common core (see Section 10, Part II). When admissions to a university degree course include those who have completed a relevant A level or GNVQ, and those who have not previously studied the subject, the problem of the starting point is even more evident. To varying degrees, students in the survey of young people's perceptions had experienced some overlap between degree courses and their A levels and GNVQs. (See Appendix B4.) High achievers at A level were much more likely to view this repetition as a hindrance.

12.66 Responding to very able students is one aspect of a wider issue with which universities are already grappling. But it is an aspect that merits their attention. The practical way forward is for universities, schools and colleges to consider local arrangements.

12.67 Some schools and more colleges are already linking more closely with higher education. This can range from university institutions offering lectures for 16–19 year olds, or allowing use of their facilities, to the study of Open University modules within schools and colleges, and individual tuition arrangements for the exceptionally able. For example, Monkseaton Community High School, Tyne and Wear, are running a pilot with the Open University for ten of their sixteen year old students to take the first year undergraduate course in Open Mathematics. There are trends within higher education that encourage the development of such links. These include: the move to modularisation within degree courses; the development of credit accumulation and transfer within both further and higher education; and the move towards local provision of higher education and open learning. A number of universities already have Associate Student Schemes which make a range of modules, including taster modules, available to students from other institutions. These modules can be taken and cashed in towards a university award at a later date. Such arrangements are available in those universities which, like Sheffield Hallam and Derby, have developed systems of credit accumulation and transfer. Many colleges of further education are already offering higher education courses (see Appendix H3).

The applied and vocational pathways

12.68 Provision above Advanced level is not yet available for young people following a predominantly GNVQ based pathway. Although the NCVQ has been consulting on introducing higher level GNVQs, these will not be available in the near future. But the structure of GNVQs allows those who progress quickly through a qualification to acquire additional units. GNVQ candidates can also broaden their studies with AS or A levels, core skill units such as problem-solving or even NVQ units. Equally, many GNVQ students will wish to progress to university courses in subjects related to their GNVQ, such as applied science, business studies, art and design. GNVQ students should have the same opportunity as A level students to benefit from local arrangements with universities to gain credit for prior learning.

12.69 The NVQ model of Modern Apprenticeships offers the most suitable exemplar for those whose interest and talents lie particularly in a vocational area, allowing them to obtain an NVQ level 3 as quickly as their talents allow. Some Modern Apprenticeship frameworks offer opportunities for young people to progress to level 4 units within their programme. This is clearly difficult in some contexts as apprenticeships will not, for example, provide the management experience required by higher level NVQs. However, where it is possible to define the knowledge and understanding required by a higher level NVQ, it should be possible for the apprentice, or adult worker, to demonstrate and secure formal certification of achievement. The Beaumont Report on the NVQ contains such proposals. Alternatively, apprentices may wish to take a related AS (for example, an AS mathematics for an engineer) or follow modules from one of the more vocationally-specific higher education courses, perhaps on a part-time or sandwich basis. Industry is increasingly forming links with the university sector to provide appropriately tailored courses for its workforce.

Extending the range of studies

12.70 The proposal in Section 8 of this Report for a new, challenging option which combines depth with breadth of study and which would be available in all three pathways, is relevant in this context.

12.71 Alternatively the young person might turn to one of a number of other programmes designed to provide breadth. Two such options may be mentioned by way of illustration. They are the General Studies at AS or A level, and the Diploma of Achievement.

12.72 The Diploma of Achievement is a new qualification awarded by the Oxford and Cambridge Schools Examination Board.[4] It is designed to occupy 10 per cent of curriculum time for four terms and to develop the skills particularly valued by employers (such as communication, numeracy, computing and team working) within a range of contexts chosen by the institution.

---

[4]   The initiative for this qualification came from Sir Ian Maclaurin at a meeting held at Malvern College in 1992. Although it originated in the independent sector, support has come from maintained schools, sixth form and FE colleges since its launch.

12.73 In contrast, the General Studies A level is well established. It has the highest take-up of any A level after mathematics and for many teachers, particularly in schools and sixth form colleges, it is a familiar and valued part of sixth form studies. There is no subject core for General Studies syllabuses to conform to, but they tend to be roughly similar. Research by the A level Information Service at Newcastle University (ALIS) indicates that General Studies is one of the hardest A levels in which to gain a high grade.

12.74 There are however problems with such options. The Diploma of Achievement is a very new award and is not recognised by all universities. Many institutions of higher education do not even value General Studies within their admissions procedure. General Studies is not subject specific, so does not carry weight with specialist admissions tutors. There is also a perception of General Studies as a subject that does not need to be taught (although this is not generally the case), and therefore some scepticism about it. Some institutions will take General Studies as a third or fourth A level, or may allow a good grade in it to compensate for a lower grade in another subject. Other admissions tutors consider it a good indicator of general ability and thus value it more highly. There is no agreed UCAS guidance on the role of General Studies.

12.75 The awarding bodies and the universities should consider the development of a General Studies A level that would be valued by all. In the light of progress made, the regulatory bodies should consider developing a subject core for General Studies to ensure that this A level develops the qualities valued by higher education and employers, including breadth, key skills and the ability to integrate different areas of knowledge. In the light of this, UCAS should, if necessary, issue guidance to ensure that General Studies plays a part in admissions procedures.

12.76 In such a General Studies A level, one possibility might be to include a module (one sixth) of an A level covering a critical approach to knowledge (see below).

A critical study of the forms of knowledge

12.77 In consultation there has been interest in a proposal for a critical examination of knowledge such as exists in the International Baccalaureate. Its purpose would be to encourage and enable students to:

■ Reflect on and question the bases of knowledge and experience.

■ Be aware of subjective and ideological biases.

■ Develop structured and logical thinking based on critical examination of evidence and expressed in rational arguments.

12.78 The course would involve:

■ Consideration of the use of language.

■ Awareness of different types of knowledge.

■ The ability to interrelate different subject areas and experiences.

■ Cultural and international understanding.

12.79 The skills assessed would include:

- *Critical thought* – quality of analysis; ability to justify argument and awareness of other points of view; awareness of the strengths and limitations of different ways of knowing; personal thought and originality.

- *Clarity* – ability to organise and structure an essay; effective use of language; ability to evaluate evidence; conceptual fluency (a skill much valued by employers as well as academics).

12.80 This course would aim to meet common concerns in universities that there is a need for students to be more rigorous in their thinking and their approach to knowledge. (One possible example of such a course is given in Appendix H2.)

12.81 It is too early to propose that this initiative should be adopted nationally. Although many further education colleges may have the capacity, the ability of the generality of schools to mount it is an issue, since it lies outside the educational tradition of England, Wales and Northern Ireland. In the International Baccalaureate it is integrated into the normal teaching of subjects. That gives it relevance and life. It would require a good deal of development by the staff of a school working together before it could be offered.

12.82 I **recommend** that this is explored by the regulatory and awarding bodies in the context of the proposed revisions to Special Papers, the new AS and the General Studies A level. This should be done in consultation with representatives of schools, colleges and institutions of higher education.

Personal development

12.83 Because of their talents, some especially able students may have difficulties in relationships with their peer group. Some may feel themselves under particular pressure to excel. Their future responsibilities will often require a robustness of personality and leadership qualities. Development of these needs to occur at the same time as development of their outstanding academic or other talents.

12.84 Only the institution can judge these issues and consider how best to foster the development of young people. Various opportunities exist both within and beyond schools and colleges. These range from participation in initiatives such as Young Enterprise or the Duke of Edinburgh's Award Scheme, to taking on leadership roles in the institution.

Summary of recommendations

12.85 Summing up, the following **recommendations** are made for young people of exceptional ability:

- Special Papers should be retained, with each awarding body agreeing to take responsibility for a number of subjects in order to secure cost-effective provision.

- Consideration should be given to developing approaches to Special Papers based on A level subject cores, which will bring them within the range of the teaching resources of more institutions.

■ Once the Special Paper has been reformulated, consideration should be given to recognising achievement through the proposed new UCAS tariff.

■ In the interests of stability a commitment should be made to provide reconstituted special papers for at least four years.

■ As an alternative to the present approach, consideration should be given to externally marked extended assignments in which students research and explain a topic or issue in depth.

■ Schools and universities should take advantage of opportunities available through arrangements such as Associate Student Schemes, to enable students to take units of university courses while at school or college. This will give them credit towards their udnergraduate studies, as well as providing an opportunity to extend their areas of interest. With such arrangements, in a few cases it may not be unrealistic to contemplate a first degree being completed in two years.

■ Schools and colleges should be encouraged to extend the range of studies available to students through additional AS or A levels, or units of GNVQs or NVQs (where appropriate opportunities can be provided) to broaden the nature of their studies. The proposal in Section 8 of this Report for a new, challenging option which combines depth with breadth of study and which would be available in all three pathways, is relevant in this context.

■ For those pursuing an NVQ, apart from taking units from another closely-related vocation, the best approach may lie in providing for certification of the underpinning knowledge and understanding required for the next level of the NVQ, or in encouraging trainees to study either an AS in a relevant area (for example, a student undertaking an NVQ level 3 in engineering might also take an AS in mathematics), or modules from a university course.

■ For GNVQ students, there are currently opportunities to take additional units at the Advanced level, or AS or A levels.

■ Consideration should be given to the content and role of a General Studies A level that will have standing with universities and attract a numerical score in the proposed new UCAS tariff.

■ An element in such a development, or a free-standing development, might be a course equivalent in weight to a Special Paper, a module or unit in a General Studies A level, or even an AS qualification, aimed at developing a critical understanding of the various forms of knowledge.

■ Students should be encouraged to pursue opportunities outside their main curriculum to develop their personal qualities through, for example, the Duke of Edinburgh's Award Scheme, Young Enterprise or work in the community.

SECTION 13

The spiritual and moral dimension of 16–19 education

13.1 Time and effort in schools and colleges are principally devoted to achievement that is formally recognised through national and other qualifications. Unless the moral and spiritual side of education is included in the framework of qualifications, there is a risk that it will get less attention than it needs for the education of young people and for the good of society in general. Maintained schools are required by the Education Reform Act to provide a curriculum which promotes the spiritual, moral, cultural, mental and physical development of pupils at the school and of society. They are also required to provide religious education to all pupils. Though further education colleges, sixth form colleges and training providers are not legally required to promote spiritual and moral development, such aspects of education are no less relevant to their students. Education about the world we live in cannot avoid moral and spiritual issues and discussion of personal qualities such as honesty, integrity and consideration for others.

13.2 Life entails a continuous series of moral judgements and decisions. In work, the need to face ethical issues arises constantly. It is increasingly recognised that companies as well as professions need to have a code of ethics. History is much concerned with human action, codes of values and the inter-play between those codes and actual behaviour. Literature is replete with ethical dilemmas and spiritual issues. Any researcher has to ensure that advocacy of a point of view not only does not compromise the dispassionate accumulation and presentation of evidence, but preferably grows from that evidence. Those in medicine and genetics are increasingly confronted with complex moral issues. New scientific developments do not simply give humans new powers, but pose new ethical problems.

13.3 The moral and spiritual dimensions are as relevant to vocational as to academic courses. Business ethics and professional conduct must be part of vocational education and training. Companies are recognising their responsibilities to their workers, for example, through Investors in People, and they are increasingly mindful of their responsibilities to the community as good corporate citizens. Environmental issues are now on the company agenda, not just as a matter of law or of the need to be sensitive to public opinion, but out of acceptance of responsibility.

13.4 Regulatory and awarding bodies should recognise the potential relevance of spiritual and moral issues to individual subjects, particularly when designing and approving syllabuses. For example, syllabuses in the sciences might include a section on the ethical dimensions of science and technology and the public understanding of science.

13.5 I recognise the weight and time many teaching institutions give to these matters. For some young people, school may be the only stable and caring community they experience. Outside the taught curriculum, much care is often given to developing pupils' moral and spiritual awareness through pastoral care. An active policy of awareness of responsibilities and rights can do much. Schools and colleges can and do transmit a common culture and common standards of citizenship. But the evidence of the times we live in suggests there is merit in re-emphasising the need to address moral and spiritual issues and to build the public and private virtues of citizenship and community.

13.6 I therefore **recommend** that:

- Regulatory and awarding bodies should recognise the potential relevance of spiritual and moral issues to individual subjects, particularly when designing and approving syllabuses.

- All providers of education and training should take spiritual and moral issues into account in the design and delivery of the curriculum and programmes for young people.

SECTION 14

Removing barriers to achievement

14.1 The Review is charged to have particular regard to the need to increase participation and achievement in education and training, and to minimise wastage. The new National Targets for Education and Training will not be achieved without success in responding to both of these requirements.

Careers education and guidance

14.2 Central to maximising achievement and reducing wastage is the provision of expert independent careers education and guidance to young people on their choice of pathways and goals. Local Education Authorities (LEAs), Training and Enterprise Council (TECs) and careers education and guidance specialists have a key role in providing this.

14.3 In a survey undertaken for the Review of young people's perceptions (see Appendix B4), over half of all students taking A level and General National Vocational Qualifications (GNVQs) said their choice of course had been influenced by a careers officer, and slightly more by teaching staff. Such official advice was felt to be a more important influence than friends or parents. The qualitative study indicated that those students who were clearer about their future plans seemed to be able to make better use of the advice and guidance provided. Where students were less sure about what they wanted, there was more likelihood of them making a rushed decision, becoming dissatisfied with their course, and subsequently realising that they had chosen subjects that did not meet their expectations.

14.4 In recognition of its importance, the 1994 and 1995 Competitiveness White Papers contained recommendations to strengthen the extent and quality of careers education and guidance. Many of these recommendations have been implemented. Both the Department for Education and Employment (DfEE) and the School Curriculum and Assessment Authority (SCAA) have produced guidance, setting out the principles of good careers education and guidance, and giving examples of how these principles can be applied[1]. There are publications of best practice for work experience for 14–19 year olds, and ACAC is due to publish guidance about setting targets to improve careers education in Wales.

14.5 Legislation proposed in the 1995 Competitiveness White Paper to require maintained schools to provide careers education will ensure that a structure is in place to improve the delivery of careers education and guidance. Meanwhile developments are underway in most local areas to define and implement quality standards for careers education and guidance. Most of these involve partnerships of schools, colleges, the Careers Service, LEAs, TECs and employers.

---

[1]   Looking forward: *Careers Education and Guidance in the Curriculum*, School Curriculum and Assessment Authority, July 1995.
A further publication to help students in making decisions is to be published in late 1996.
Better Choices: Working Together to Improve Careers Education and Guidance: Principles into Practice Employment Department/Department for Education, 1995

14.6 Rapid economic and technological change is having a dramatic effect on the development of career opportunities. The experience and knowledge of those providing the careers education and guidance must be kept up to date. TECs, Education Business Partnerships and the Teacher Placement Programme have a key role to play, and it would be helpful if there were greater consistency in their activities in informing those giving careers guidance about developments in Modern Apprenticeships, GNVQs and National Vocational Qualifications (NVQs).

14.7 Now that the framework for careers education and guidance is largely in place, emphasis should be placed on the careers educators in schools and colleges and on the Careers Service advisers working together to give every student a co-ordinated programme of careers education and guidance.

The need for better information

14.8 There are at present too many unexplained gaps between the number of candidates registering for qualifications, and the number successfully completing them. Data is not collected reliably or consistently at a national or local level. There may be good and positive reasons for non-completion (for example, success in obtaining a job), but there are many instances where non-completion cannot be satisfactorily explained.[2]

14.9 Action to maximise achievement depends on good information about the reasons for students not completing courses, and about influences on students' decisions.

14.10 Research carried out by the Further Education Development Agency (FEDA) on non-completion indicates that those who leave early are much more likely than those who stay the course to feel dissatisfied with the quality of teaching and the support they get from the institution. (See Appendix B3.)

14.11 Several reports which have included recommendations for the improvement of retention rates suggest that schools and colleges should target attention on the following areas.

■ Ensuring students are entered on an appropriate course.

■ Improving induction and support.

■ Making changes to courses and monitoring student progress.

■ Identifying and helping students at risk of withdrawal, and improving management information systems[3]. (See Appendix B1.)

14.12 However, to monitor achievement, high-quality, continuously-updated information is needed both at the level of individual institutions and nationally for action to be taken. Present arrangements do not appear to be adequate and I **recommend** that they are reviewed.

---

[2] The NFER research study *Completion of A level and GNVQ Courses in Schools* found that 7 per cent of students withdrew from the first year of one or more A levels and 2 per cent withdrew in the second year. The study also found that in the first year of Advanced GNVQ 17 per cent withdrew, and 8 per cent withdrew in the second year. (See Appendix B2.)

[3] The NFER report *Completion of A level and GNVQ Courses: a literature review.* (See Appendix B1.)

Gender issues

14.13 The balance of performance between boys and girls has changed over recent years. Girls out-perform boys in National Curriculum assessments in England, and this pattern continues to GCSE. The pattern of GCSE achievement is illustrated by the following table.

Table 15 Percentages of Year 11 cohort awarded five or more GCSE grades A*–C

	1988	1989	1990	1991	1992	1993	1994
Girls	31.7	35.8	38.4	40.3	42.7	45.8	47.8
Boys	28.2	29.8	30.8	33.3	34.1	36.8	39.1

14.14 The pattern of performance in GCSE across the sexes is consistent when comparisons are made by types of schools.

Table 16 GCSE performance analysed by sex, all secondary schools (excluding special schools)

School Type[4]	Number of Schools	Average GCSE points score		
		Boys	**Girls**	**All**
Mixed with 6th form	1458	31.4	35.7	33.6
Mixed without 6th form	1272	28.7	33.0	30.8

14.15 It is not that performance by boys has deteriorated, but that performance by girls has improved more rapidly. The distinctly greater improvement in girls' performance has been a substantial factor in the overall improvement in GCSE results in the last seven years.

14.16 At A level also, performance by girls has improved more quickly than that of boys. Boys do remain slightly ahead overall, and comparative performance varies by subject area. For example, at grades A–B in 1994, girls out-performed boys in Art and Design, Geography, and Home Economics. Boys performed better in General Studies, Computing and Business Studies.

14.17 There has been some debate about whether different modes of assessment, and the nature of what is being assessed, favour males and females differentially. For example, there has been a suggestion that girls perform better at coursework than in examinations. This is not supported by research, at least in English and mathematics. It is also argued that questions in English tend to require reflective, empathetic and

---

4   Data are available for all types of schools, and show consistent patterns. Mixed schools with sixth forms are chosen for illustration.

biographic skills which girls find more congenial, whereas boys prefer a more factual documentary approach. At higher levels there is a suggestion that the allegedly male traits of speculation and assertive argument may be more highly valued than careful argument based on evidence, which may be more characteristic of females.

14.18 The change in the relative performance of the genders must be a matter for continuing research to ensure that all students achieve their full potential, and that their achievements are recognised. The next major review of the National Curriculum will provide an opportunity to review the extent to which the National Curriculum and the GCSE give boys and girls equal opportunity to demonstrate their skills.

14.19 Too few young women are following programmes in engineering, the physical sciences and technology. In 1993 a committee appointed by the Government produced a report on women in science, engineering and technology, *The Rising Tide*. This made a range of proposals for increasing female participation in these subject areas and observed that if most young women are choosing only three subjects, as in the typical A level programme, they may be less willing to take risks in their choices. An option at 16, as canvassed in Section 8 of this Report, to pursue a broader range of subjects, could encourage more young women to consider continued study in the sciences.

14.20 Figures from Scotland, where a wider range of subjects is commonly pursued in the first year of sixth form study, offer support for this view. For example, whereas in Scotland twice as many boys as girls take physics, in England nearly four times as many boys as girls take this subject. Whereas in Scotland take-up of mathematics is fairly even (53 per cent of boys as compared to 47 per cent of girls), in England nearly twice as many boys take mathematics as girls.

14.21 Figures on the take-up of GNVQ by gender (see Appendix J1) show a very traditional pattern of choices. Similarly, in the Modern Apprenticeships, at this early stage, young men outnumber young women by 3:1, reflecting the historical gender stereotypes of desired occupations and the concentration of the early Modern Apprenticeship schemes in traditional male industry sectors. These are tendencies that merit consideration if the full potential of young women is to be realised. In Wales, a target has been set to encourage girls to enter Modern Apprenticeships in manufacturing.

Ethnic issues

14.22 During the Review concern has been expressed that there is insufficient understanding of the extent to which those for whom English is an additional language are handicapped in examinations by the difficulties they may have in understanding the precise meaning of questions, and the time they may spend in working out what is required.

14.23 Research by FEDA has looked into cultural and linguistic factors affecting GNVQ assessment. This has indicated the high level of language skills required to achieve awards. It has also noted that certain forms of assessment disadvantage some people from cultural backgrounds who may find that the GNVQ (and NVQ) assessment model does not reward them for factual knowledge, in contrast to their previous experience where success has been achieved through examinations. Ethnic minority students, particularly girls, were found to have difficulties with programmes where group work and investigations required assertive behaviour and independent decision making.

14.24 The research identified a number of relevant points, including the need to:

- Review the language involved in GNVQ specifications to minimise potential barriers to understanding.

- Clarify grading themes and criteria.

- Engage students in active debate about assessment issues.

- Provide appropriate language and learning support.

- Ensure as far as possible that the timing of assessment or final examinations does not disadvantage certain groups of students (for example by coinciding with religious festivals).

Socio-economic group

14.25 Certain features of qualification design may assist in motivating learners who have little background of educational achievement. For example, the possibility of securing recognition for achievement through units in the GNVQ and NVQ, or through modules in A levels, is a good form of motivation for those who live in an environment where the future is uncertain and there are low levels of confidence and self-esteem. This issue of the need to find motivating approaches to learning, whether within or outside the National Curriculum, is central to achievement by those who are unsuccessful, whatever their socio-economic group. That point is taken up in Section 12 dealing with lower attainers.

14.26 The table in Appendix J2 suggests that there is a strong correlation between socio-economic group (if eligibility for free school meals is taken as an indicator) and GCSE results, although it should be noted that schools with similar socio-economic backgrounds can perform very differently at GCSE and A level. Nevertheless, low performance by working class boys is increasingly emerging as an issue for concern. Though no evidence was presented to the Review to suggest that the nature or content of qualifications for 16–19 year olds could be a factor in this, we must be sensitive to the need to ensure that the framework of qualifications does not compound disadvantage.

Disability

14.27 Candidates with learning difficulties and disabilities have arguably faced more barriers than most in their progress towards qualifications (particularly through the specification of qualifications), in the area of work experience, and in the availability of arrangements for special assignments.

14.28 Special arrangements for learners with disabilities are not always consistent across the qualification pathways. Awarding bodies have different requirements and will make different arrangements for candidates. Within the same qualification route, different programmes may also be inconsistent. For instance, whereas NVQ Business Administration allows hearing-impaired candidates to demonstrate telephone skills using a minicom system, the NVQ in Hairdressing does not permit use of a minicom. Although revisions of the specifications have helped, NCVQ units in communication, the application of number and information technology still present problems. For example, in the application of number, information presented in a visual format with diagrams cannot always be presented in alternative ways, so some units cannot be achieved by blind and visually impaired candidates.

14.29 NCVQ's Access and Fair Assessment Advisory Forum has recently shown how the words used to describe learners and their needs can be discouraging and act as a barrier to access and assessment. Proposals have already been made to respond to this. The Tomlinson Committee[5] advocates an approach which recognises the needs of individual learners.

14.30 Common approaches to approval, quality assurance and assessment would reduce such inconsistencies. All awarding bodies are alert to these issues and are committed to eliminating barriers. Concerted efforts are now needed by the regulatory and awarding bodies to remove barriers within qualifications and assessment to improve access to learning opportunities for disabled people. The regulatory bodies should consider access to qualifications as part of their work on quality assurance, particularly when they approve and monitor qualifications. Proposals are included in the recommendations at the end of this section.

Countering stereotypes

14.31 The FEDA survey (Appendix B3) illustrates that the qualifications framework alone will not redress patterns of under-achievement. The quality of student-teacher relationships and of the learning experience, and the way in which expectations are shaped by stereotypes, are influential factors.

14.32 Young people often have in their minds stereotypes of suitable and realistic ways forward, whether in education or work. Such stereotypes may help to sustain patterns of under-achievement by race, class, gender and disability. Stereotyping by gender has been substantially eroded in the GCSE (possibly as a result of the common framework of the National Curriculum), and is illustrated by the improvement in achievement by girls in subjects where boys have hitherto done better. But it persists at the higher levels, particularly where vocations and vocational courses are being chosen. Those from less favoured backgrounds may have stereotyped concepts of what may be feasible options for them, based on family experience and expectations. These are issues which those giving careers education and guidance need to have in mind. The Equal Opportunities Commission has agreed the specification for training of Careers Service staff so that the advice they provide to young people, and to employers about placements, is non-discriminatory and does not reinforce stereotyped occupational choices.

Opportunities for work experience

14.33 Demonstration of full competence for vocational awards is limited at present by a shortage of opportunities for work experience for potential candidates, and by limited access to work experience for those who are employed but seeking to develop broader skills. For those in work, the problems are aggravated by the lack of continuity of opportunity often caused by short-term contracts. People with disabilities, who have even greater difficulty than most in finding work or work experience, may find that the new Disability Discrimination Bill and Access to Work programmes improve their chances in the longer term.

---

[5] The Committee on learning difficulties and disabilities set up by the Further Education Funding Council under the chairmanship of Professor John Tomlinson.

14.34 Although simulation offers a useful and necessary route it is not, as recent research has shown, a full answer. Real working relationships and contingencies are difficult to replicate. Wider access to qualifications may therefore depend on a considerable expansion of opportunities for work experience or a development of simulation techniques. Appropriate guidance, resources and learning support at key transition points, particularly for those whose work experience may be limited or interrupted, are also needed. In their own interests, all companies should see what more they can do to provide opportunities for work experience.

Recommendations

14.35 To increase participation and achievement in education and training, to remove barriers to access, and to reduce wastage, I **recommend** that:

- Excellent, independent careers education and guidance should be provided to all young people on their choice of pathways and on their potential level of achievement, recognising the central role of local partnerships between schools, colleges and the careers service. Continued updating of knowledge should be provided to those giving advice, including issues relevant to maintaining equal opportunities.

- The regulatory, awarding and industry lead bodies should consider the issues relating to access to qualifications as part of their work on quality assurance, including:

  - the specification of content (audit of content for clarity, cultural and linguistic bias);

  - assessment arrangements (special arrangements, preparation and timing of assessments);

  - guidance to centres (for example on equipment and learning support).

- Awarding bodies should include criteria on accessibility and training in related issues as part of revised Codes of Practice and centre approval criteria.

- Regulatory, awarding and lead bodies should continue to review the extent to which the content and arrangements for all forms of assessment need to be designed in ways that maintain standards but give equality of opportunity for all to demonstrate their achievement, independent of gender, racial origin, socio-economic group or disability, with research being commissioned as required to verify that there are no unnecessary obstacles to achievement.

- The regulatory bodies (and other appropriate agencies) should work together to develop a framework for monitoring and reporting nationally on candidate achievement by gender, racial origin, socio-economic group, disability or learning difficulty.

- The Government departments, regulatory and awarding bodies, Further Education Funding Councils, FEDA and other appropriate bodies should further investigate reasons for non-completion of awards (including the influence of external factors such as financial pressures, employment circumstances, personal problems, and the quality of the learning experience). They should improve the reliability of information on completion and destinations of all leavers.

■ The regulatory bodies should explore (with employer bodies, Government departments and others) ways of encouraging an expansion of work experience opportunities.

■ Schools and colleges should maximise the potential of information technology to improve their monitoring and tracking of students.

SECTION 15

Action

15.1 Schools, colleges and providers of training have experienced unprecedented change in recent years. So, too, have the regulatory and awarding bodies for whom the recommendations in this Report will also involve significant additional effort if coherence is to be achieved. It is with all of these in mind that I **recommend** the following.

- The recommendations in this Report to strengthen qualifications are interdependent with those of the Capey Committee and of the Beaumont Review. Action on these recommendations should be co-ordinated by Government departments to minimise the burden on institutions, the awarding bodies and providers of education and training.

- In the light of the Government's response to this Report, the Department for Education and Employment (DfEE), Welsh Office and Northern Ireland Office should consult with the regulatory and awarding bodies, other Government departments and the inspectorates, Further Education Funding Councils (England and Wales), Further Education Development Agency and the Teacher Training Agency on the implications of the Report and on a joint agenda for action.

- In recognition of the emphasis placed by all parties in consultation upon the need to raise national standards in the key skills of communication, the application of number and information technology, and the value attached by employers to personal and inter-personal skills, these should be included in the priorities in the joint agenda for action.

- With the continued growth of post-16 education and training, and the wider range of opportunities being offered in the applied and vocational pathways, consideration will need to be given at all levels to the curriculum that schools and colleges of different sizes can realistically provide and manage effectively within the resources available.

15.2 The recommendations in this Report have been made to raise achievement, to reduce wastage and secure good value for money. But all change involves some initial costs, particularly in terms of human effort and commitment. This is especially so in the education and training of teachers: but nowhere is it more important to invest.

15.3 My final proposals therefore relate to teacher quality. The Teacher Training Agency has identified the 14–19 phase as a national priority in its recent review of continuing professional development, and is working on developing national standards to underpin the award of Qualified Teacher Status. The Government has also announced the setting up of a Further Education Staff Development Forum, supported by FEDA, with a remit to develop national standards and a framework for continuing professional development in the further education sector. I **recommend** further consideration of the following points.

■ The case for more specific criteria for courses of initial teacher training which cover the 14–19 phase in schools.

■ The implications of this Report for programmes of in-service education and training for teachers in schools.

■ Whether, in the light of the outcome of the deliberations of the Further Education Staff Development Forum, there is scope for further measures for the initial and continuing training of teachers and trainers not in schools.

S E C T I O N 1 6

List of recommendations

A national framework of qualifications

1   There should be a National Framework of Qualifications. All qualifications in the national framework will be allocated to four **National levels** known as Advanced, Intermediate, Foundation and Entry level. (Section 3.8.)

2   The term **National** should characterise all the main elements in the framework envisaged in the Report[1]. These include National Awards, National Record of Achievement, National Traineeships, National Certificates, National Advanced Diploma and National Vocational Qualifications. (Section 3.9.)

3   All certificates issued by awarding bodies should show the relevant national level prominently as the main heading. To assist understanding of what has been achieved, the new certificates should include (on the reverse side) a list of the main comparable nationally recognised achievements at the relevant level. The face of the certificate should give more detail than at present about the nature of the achievement. For certificates at the Advanced level, provision should be made for including the numerical score based on the proposed new Universities and Colleges Admissions Service (UCAS) tariff. A certificate number should be included on each certificate. (Section 3.13.)

4   National criteria should be developed in order to recognise and formally ascribe national levels to other current major qualifications which fall outside the three main qualifications pathways. (Section 3.13.)

5   The form of the new certificates should be as illustrated at the end of Section 3. (Section 3.13.)

6   The distinguishing characteristics appropriate to each pathway should reflect the underlying purpose, as outlined below.

■ **A level and GCSE** – where the primary purpose is to develop knowledge, understanding and skills associated with a subject or discipline.

■ **Applied education (GNVQ)** – where the primary purpose is to develop and apply knowledge, understanding and skills relevant to broad areas of employment.

■ **Vocational training (NVQ)** – where the primary purpose is to develop and recognise mastery of a trade or profession at the relevant level. (Section 3.24.)

7   Below A level, it should be accepted that the GCSE develops general education as well as the practical application of skills, for example in communication and the application of number. But in subject areas outside the National Curriculum, or where GCSE subject-specific criteria do not already exist, studies in the practical applications of knowledge and understanding relevant to broad areas of employment should normally be regarded as the province of the GNVQ, unless there are good reasons to the contrary. (Section 3.26.)

8   The joint committee of the NCVQ and SCAA proposed in Section 4 should enter into discussion with the awarding bodies and recommend broad principles for allocating subject areas to pathways, for the approval of the Secretaries of State. (Section 3.27.)

9   The joint committee should consider all proposals for new awards and programmes, and make recommendations to the parent bodies. As qualifications come forward for revision and approval, their appropriateness for a particular pathway should be reviewed. (Section 3.27.)

10   The joint committee might also consider whether in the longer term there is a case for a national subject framework for qualifications based on coherent groupings of broad subject areas. (Section 3.27.)

[1]   It is for consideration to what extent in Wales these should be identified as 'Welsh National'.

11   In the light of the outcome of the Gatsby project, awarding bodies should examine the scope for identifying common content in related areas of study in modular A levels and GNVQs, bearing in mind the feasibility of common elements being taught together, but without changing the distinctive nature and rigour of each of these qualifications. (Section 3.37.)

12   The joint committee of the NCVQ and SCAA should, in consultation with centres, awarding bodies and representatives of higher education and employment, oversee the development of a common framework for the quality assurance of all national qualifications. (Section 3.43.)

13   The committee should take into account the extent to which a common framework (of quality assurance) might recognise the distinctive features of qualifications and avoid compromising them. (Section 3.43.)

14   These arrangements should include common timetables for the review, development and approval of qualifications in related subject areas. (Section 3.43.)

15   These arrangements should cover the development and approval of syllabuses, the roles of centres, awarding and regulatory bodies in assessment, recording, grading, moderation, monitoring, and centre approval. (Section 3.43.)

16   Awarding bodies should be encouraged to revise codes of practice in the light of the common quality assurance framework. (Section 3.43.)

17   Particular attention should be paid to how these arrangements might apply to the development and approval of NVQs and work-based training such as Modern Apprenticeships, and the new initiatives to replace Youth Training which are proposed in Section 5. (Section 3.43.)

18   In developing its proposals the joint committee should consider ways of increasing the cost effectiveness and reducing the workload in schools and colleges. (Section 3.43)

19   The joint committee of the NCVQ and SCAA should take forward the development of a common vocabulary which should be adopted by the regulatory and awarding bodies for all qualifications. (Section 3.47.)

20   The regulatory bodies should commit themselves to using plain words in all their publications. (Section 3.47.)

The regulatory and awarding bodies

21   The Government departments should encourage awarding bodies to come together across the binary line to create new joint arrangements for awarding the GCSE, A level and GNVQ. (Section 4.30.)

22   The Government departments should, at the same time, take action to rationalise:

   ■   the number of bodies involved in the awarding of qualifications;

   ■   the number of NVQ awarding bodies. (Section 4.30.)

23   Legislation should be introduced to bring together the work of the NCVQ and SCAA.

24   To that end the Government should consult on the following alternatives:

   ■   bringing together all the work of the NCVQ and SCAA into one single statutory body, or

   ■   regrouping the qualifications and public examinations functions of the NCVQ and SCAA into a new National Qualifications Authority, with a separate authority responsible for the school curriculum from 4–19, for statutory assessment up to the age of 14, and possibly, in the interests of reducing the number of bodies involved in education, for some other functions. (Section 4.30.)

25 The consultation should further consider how employment interests might best be represented in future arrangements in order to ensure that NVQs continue to be based on occupational standards and remain employment-led. (Section 4.30.)

26 In the event of legislation, specific provision should be made for Wales and Northern Ireland. (Section 4.30.)

27 In the meantime, the Government should support the co-ordinating work of the joint committee of the NCVQ and SCAA, with the full involvement of Wales and Northern Ireland. (Section 4.30.)

28 The Welsh Office and the Department for Education in Northern Ireland, together with ACAC, CCEA and their English counterparts, should consider which structure would best preserve the responsiveness and distinctiveness of the present arrangements, while progressing towards removing the academic/vocational divide. (Section 4.32.)

29 The regulatory bodies in Wales and Northern Ireland (ACAC and CCEA) should not extend their roles to cover policy towards and accreditation of, the NVQ. (Section 4.35.)

30 Further consideration should now be given as a matter of urgency, to ACAC taking responsibility for the GNVQ framework in Wales. (Section 4.35.)

31 The CCEA in Northern Ireland and the WJEC in Wales should move into offering GNVQs, through association with one or more of the existing GNVQ awarding bodies. (Section 4.35.)

32 Arrangements should be made to provide for Wales and Northern Ireland to take part in the work of any new bodies established to undertake the present work of the NCVQ and SCAA, and meanwhile they will be represented on the joint committee of the NCVQ and SCAA. (Section 4.35.)

Youth Training and Modern Apprenticeships

33 Youth Training, however currently named, should be relaunched as a system of **National Traineeships,** available at **Foundation, Intermediate,** and perhaps at **Advanced levels,** providing a vocational progression route to Modern Apprenticeships and the work-based route. (Section 5.14.)

34 **National Traineeships** should offer a broad and flexible learning programme for young people, designed by Industry Training Organisations (ITOs) and TECs and delivered in partnership with colleges of further education. Each Traineeship should incorporate NVQs (at levels 1, 2 and perhaps 3 as appropriate to the industry), the three key skills of communication, the application of number and information technology and (where appropriate) units, short courses and whole qualifications, such as GNVQs and GCSEs. (Section 5.14.)

35 Acceptance to a National Traineeship should be based on an assessment of the applicant's suitability. It should not be the fall-back position for young people without a job. (Section 5.14.)

36 For those not yet ready for NVQ level 1, including those with special training needs and those unclear about their career direction, **National Entry level provision** should be developed, geared towards the Entry level qualifications proposed in this Report (see Section 12), and available through a range of motivating vocational contexts. (Section 5.14.)

37 The National Entry level provision should foster the development of the three key skills of communication, the application of number and information technology including self-expression, and handling an interview... (Section 5.14.)

38 LEAs, TECs, the Careers Service, schools, colleges and other organisations with experience in developing provision at this level should be involved in developing and managing the National Entry level provision. Opportunities for links with college and school-based initiatives for the Entry level group should be explored, in order to bring coherence locally to education and work-based provision. (Section 5.14.)

39 As with Modern Apprenticeships, applicants for National Traineeships and the National Entry level provision should be required to enter into an agreement with the training provider/TEC, perhaps brokered by the Careers Service, outlining the responsibilities of both the individual and the provider. (Section 5.14.)

40 Clear routes of progression should be established so that young people can readily progress up the levels of the National Traineeship and into Modern Apprenticeships, college-based provision or jobs as appropriate. (Section 5.14.)

41 To help young people take full advantage of available progression opportunities and to continue their development, all should receive support in drawing up a career and training plan when they start and when they leave National Traineeships and the National Entry level provision. (Section 5.14.)

42 Quality assurance arrangements for National Traineeships should be developed consistent with those for the Modern Apprenticeships. Given the different features of the National Entry level provision, arrangements may differ at this level. All quality assurance arrangements should be closely linked to arrangements in other pathways. (Section 5.14.)

43 Appropriate arrangements should be devised for funding TECs to contribute with local partners to the National Entry level provision. (Section 5.14.)

44 Consideration should be given to reformulating the Government guarantee to those not in full-time education or employment in the light of proposals for National Traineeships and the National Entry level provision. Decisions on the appropriate provision for any individual should be based on a careful assessment of their training needs. (Section 5.14.)

45 Schools and the Careers Service should be well briefed so that young people have the Modern Apprenticeship option presented to them. (Section 5.23.)

46 Employers should ensure that apprenticeships provide not only the necessary skills, but sufficient underpinning knowledge and understanding to enable Modern Apprentices, having obtained the NVQ level 3, to go on if they wish to part-time, full-time, or sandwich courses leading to diplomas and degrees. (Section 5.23.)

47 Progression routes should be defined to make it easier for young people who have attained relevant GNVQs in full-time education to progress to Modern Apprenticeships and NVQs. (Section 5.23.)

48 Employers taking on Modern Apprentices should plan their deployment on the completion of the apprenticeship to ensure that momentum is not lost. (Section 5.23.)

49 Participation and achievement for males and females, and people from minority ethnic groups, should be monitored at national, regional and industry sector levels. (Section 5.23.)

50 Monitoring should be undertaken to identify whether the vocational route is being seen by young people as a means of accessing higher education, and whether qualified apprentices are being offered full-time or part-time university places on completion of their Modern Apprenticeships. (Section 5.23.)

51 While recognising that the focus lies with 16–17 year olds, there should be research into ways of addressing the balance of provision among 16–25 year olds. (Section 5.23.)

The National Record of Achievement

52 With the support of employers, the NRA should be reviewed and relaunched, possibly under a new name which would reflect its wider role in personal development. (Section 6.21.)

53 The NRA should have a major role in developing skills in planning and managing one's own learning through a self-contained section, based on specially designed worksheets, which guides the student through the process. The section should be worked out in consultation with schools and colleges... (Section 6.21.)

54   During 16–19 education and training, consideration should be given to assessing and certificating young people's skills in planning and managing their own learning. This could be done through NCVQ's unit, 'improving own learning and performance'... (Section 6.21.)

55   The NRA should be introduced when decisions are being taken about the last two years of statutory schooling, say at $13^1/_2$ years rather than at 16. The present quality folder provided by the Government should be available to students at that age. (Section 6.21.)

56   Use of the NRA throughout lifetime learning should be strongly encouraged and supported by the Government, employers, LEAs, TECs, schools, colleges, universities and other institutions. (Section 6.21.)

57   Use of the NRA as a tool for lifetime learning should be encouraged through Investors in People. (Section 6.21.)

58   All students should receive guidance from schools and colleges on using the NRA in applying for a university places, jobs, and in interviews. (Section 6.21.)

59   Consideration should be given to making the NRA processes of recording achievement and action planning part of the schools' and colleges' inspection frameworks. (Section 6.21.)

60   The existing 'Qualifications and Credits' sheet in the NRA should be entitled the 'Record of National Awards' to record all qualifications and units recognised at national level as part of the national framework outlined in Section 3 of this Report. (Section 6.21.)

Improving skills for work and lifetime learning

61   To underline the importance of number, the regulatory and awarding bodies should provide a separate grading for those aspects of GCSE mathematics concerned with calculation, estimation, and statistics. This grade would be shown separately on the face of the certificate. This would complement the recent proposal by the Secretaries of State to give a separate grading for spoken English and Welsh alongside the overall grade for the GCSE in these subjects. (Section 7.24.)

62   In information technology (for which a range of full, combined or short course GCSEs and other vocational qualifications already exist, but none of which is necessarily taken by all students) the NCVQ units in information technology should be approved as a basis for assessment at Key Stage 4 in schools. Schools should be encouraged to offer appropriate information technology qualifications to all pupils. (Section 7.24.)

63   The A level subject cores and syllabuses should be reviewed by the appropriate regulatory awarding bodies to identify what further scope there is to build in relevant elements in communication, the application of number and information technology without distorting the integrity of individual subjects. (Section 7.27.)

64   The three key skill units required in GNVQs offer one way of recognising these achievements. In addition to this, students should have the opportunity to develop their key skills by taking a new 'AS in key skills'. The level of performance in each of the skills of communication, the application of number, and information technology would be separately recognised in the award, and contribute to the overall grade. A minimum level of achievement in each skill would be required for an award. (Section 7.29.)

65   The proposal for a new AS in key skills is not made as a mandatory requirement for the award of A levels, but to encourage students to recognise that these skills are essential for work and adult life, regardless of the qualifications pathway followed between 16 and 19. I see this new AS as a major element in the proposals from this Review. The majority of students should be encouraged to seek it; universities should make clear that they value it; employers should make it a specific issue in their recruitment; and it should provide a way of satisfying the mandatory requirements for the new certificate and diploma recommended in Section 8. (Section 7.30.)

66   The joint committee of the NCVQ and SCAA proposed in Section 4 of this Report should review the present requirements for the three key skills in the Advanced level in the GNVQ, with a view to considering the extent to which there should be common standards for the GNVQ and the proposed new AS in key skills.... The essence of the award would lie in the skills being demonstrated in a context

broadly relevant to the main areas of knowledge covered by A levels. To provide context, perhaps 40 per cent of the marks might be available from coursework arising from the student's A level work, with the remaining 60 per cent depending upon examination, contextualised so far as possible for the main areas of knowledge. (Section 7.31.)

67 The views of employers and universities on the key skills should be taken into account in the work of the NCVQ/SCAA joint committee. (Section 7.35.)

68 The NCVQ should consider the use of appropriately designed, simple-to-use tests for components of the units in communication, the application of number and information technology. These tests should be varied enough to meet a wide range of interests. Such tests could provide a common element between the NCVQ units and the proposed AS in key skills. (Section 7.37.)

69 Beyond the lowest rungs of the NVQ ladder, skills in communication and the application of number become an increasingly necessary competence. By the time candidates are approaching NVQ level 3, reaching the supervisory level in work terms, these skills are becoming more relevant, and they should be included. I therefore recommend further discussion with the lead bodies for the various sections of industry, the awarding bodies and the NCVQ, to assess the case for their explicit inclusion in the specifications where they are an essential requirement for the job. (Section 7.41.)

70 All schools, colleges, and training bodies that receive public funding to provide education and training for 16–19 year olds (including Youth Training, the new National Traineeships and National Entry level provision and Modern Apprenticeships), should provide opportunities for all young people to develop these skills and to have them assessed. Wherever practicable, such learning should be related to the kind of experience the young person is likely to have in his or her work. (Section 7.42.)

71 All young people on programmes funded at public expense should be required to take advantage of the facilities offered for developing the key skills. (Section 7.43.)

72 This commitment to developing key skills should be identified as a priority in the development plans of those institutions and monitored by the appropriate regulatory and inspection bodies. (Section 7.44.)

73 All those seeking awards in the proposed National Certificates and Diplomas (see Section 8) would need to achieve standards in the three key skills through either the proposed AS in key skills or the NCVQ units in communication, the application of number and information technology at level 3. (Section 7.45.)

74 Universities and employers should be urged to make a particular point of making clear to candidates that acquisition of the new AS in key skills (or the NCVQ equivalent) will bear on their recruitment decisions. (Section 7.45.)

75 Teachers will need help and guidance through programmes of staff development to enable them to provide opportunities for the further development of key skills within A level courses and to prepare them for teaching the new AS in key skills. (Section 7.45.)

76 All learners, including A level students, should be given opportunities by institutions to practise making oral presentations to peer groups, to engage in discussion on their presentations, and to tackle projects through group work to develop their experience of team working. (Section 7.52.)

77 Learners should be encouraged to record their achievements in these skills in their National Record of Achievement and to gain certification through NCVQ units in 'improving own learning and performance' and 'working with others' post-16. (Section 7.52.)

78 Institutions should be encouraged to identify opportunities for developing learners' personal and inter-personal skills in their development plans, and this should be monitored by inspection bodies. (Section 7.52.)

National Targets, National Certificates and the National Advanced Diploma

79   A National Certificate should be introduced to recognise achievement at the Intermediate and Advanced levels. The requirements for each level should be as follows:

■   **Intermediate level:** a minimum of 5 GCSEs at grade C or above, including English or Welsh, mathematics, and the full, combined-subject or short course GCSE in information technology; or a GNVQ at Intermediate level; or a full NVQ at level 2. Where GCSEs in English or Welsh, mathematics and information technology have not been achieved at grade C or above, competence must be demonstrated in the NCVQ units of communication, the application of number and information technology at level 2. (Section 8.15.)

■   **Advanced level:** two A level passes, or a full GNVQ at the Advanced level, or a full NVQ at level 3, plus competence in communication, the application of number and information technology demonstrated through the NCVQ units at level 3 or through the new AS in the three key skills these being harmonised to be of the same standard. (Section 8.15.)

80   Consideration should be given to the creation of a National Certificate at the Foundation level... (Section 8.15.)

81   Work should be carried out to identify those other major awards which should count for recognition towards the achievement of the National Certificate at the Intermediate and Advanced levels. (Section 8.15.)

82   The National Certificate should be designed to recognise achievement over and above the minimum requirements for the award. (Section 8.15.)

83   The Government should work with LEAs, TECs and other relevant partners to ensure that the setting, monitoring and achievement of local targets is consistent with, and contributes to, the National Targets for Education and Training. (Section 8.15.)

84   In addition LEAs, TECs and the Further Education Funding Councils should work with locally managed and grant maintained schools and colleges on setting, monitoring and achieving institutional targets linked to the National Certificates. (Section 8.15.)

85   The Government should consider the case for governing bodies of schools and colleges to report on progress against institutional targets as part of the annual report to parents and the wider community. (Section 8.15.)

86   The National Certificates should be issued by schools and colleges and for those at work, by TECs, on the basis of awards made by the awarding bodies, with strong arrangements to ensure tight control over the granting of certificates and safeguards against fraudulent practice. (Section 8.15.)

87   A distinctive diploma at Advanced level should be created to recognise achievement in studies both in depth and in breadth to be known as the National Advanced Diploma ('The Diploma'). (Section 8.64.)

88   The heart of this award would be two full A levels *or* a full Advanced GNVQ, *or* a full NVQ at level 3, *or* agreed equivalents. (Section 8.64.)

89   Breadth would be provided by studies in complementary areas so that between the studies in depth and those in breadth, four broadly defined areas of study would be covered to the minimum of the new AS proposed in Section 11. For A level students, these areas might be defined as:

■   science, technology, engineering and mathematics;

■   modern languages (including Welsh for students for whom it is not their first language);

■   the arts and humanities (including English and Welsh); and

■   the way the community works (including business, economics, government and politics, law, psychology and sociology). (Section 8.64.)

90   For the GNVQ and NVQ a complementary approach would be needed, based on coherent groupings of units from subject areas other than the main study, which would include a modern language. (Section 8.64.)

91   Studies in supporting areas would need to be at least an AS qualification, or the equivalent, in terms of units from the GNVQ or NVQ. (Section 8.64.)

92   In addition, all those seeking this Diploma would need to achieve the three key skills through either the proposed AS in key skills or the NCVQ units in communication, the application of number and information technology at level 3, these being harmonised to be of the same standard. (Section 8.64.)

93   The National Advanced Diploma should be issued by schools and colleges on the basis of certificates issued by the national awarding bodies, personally signed by the head of the institution. When that is not possible, they should be awarded by any body authorised to award A levels or GNVQs, on the basis of certificates, and on a payment of a fee to cover administration costs. (Section 8.64.)

94   For candidates proceeding through the NVQ pathway, the National Advanced Diploma would be issued by TECs, or by any of the authorised awarding bodies on payment of a fee, following confirmation of the underpinning certificates. (Section 8.64.)

The GNVQ, NVQ and other vocational qualifications

95   Part One GNVQ at the Foundation and Intermediate levels, as it is called, is a self-standing qualification which meets the needs of 14–16 year olds, and can be accommodated alongside the statutory National Curriculum requirements at Key Stage 4. It should be made available for use by 16–19 year olds and subject to experience with the pilots. (Section 9.11.)

96   The title 'Applied A level' should replace GNVQ (Advanced level), and this term should be adopted on all awarding certificates. (Section 9.16.)

97   Because of the size of the full GNVQ and the desirability of building up a common structure with A level, GNVQ should be structured and named such that the full GNVQ of 12 units, plus the three NCVQ key skill units is called the **Applied A level (Double Award)** and the proposed six unit GNVQ plus the three NCVQ key skill units is called the **Applied A level**. (Section 9.16.)

98   Detailed consideration should also be given to the creation of a three unit GNVQ award to be known as the **Applied AS,** to match the AS in the A level family. (Section 9.16.)

99   Further consultation should be undertaken to establish whether the GNVQs at Intermediate and Foundation levels, and Part One GNVQs, should be renamed. Proposals for consultation could include the names 'Applied Intermediate levels' and 'Applied Foundation levels'. (Section 9.16.)

100   In the Part One GNVQ, and more widely where it would help, the required knowledge and understanding should be stated in the specifications for GNVQs or in the guidance to teachers. (Section 9.17.)

101   In the expansion of the GNVQ into new institutions, and as new subjects are introduced into institutions, the NCVQ and the awarding bodies should maintain rigorous policies to ensure that there is the necessary expertise and equipment. (Section 9.17.)

102   Guidance to students on GNVQ choices should avoid gender stereotyping and be based on individual considerations of suitability, the scope for progression and prospects. (Section 9.17.)

103   In subjects like manufacturing and engineering, where equipment is costly, the Government should be alert to the possibility that take-up could be unreasonably constrained across the country, with the consequence that student and institutional choice is concentrated too heavily on the comparatively low-cost service sectors. (Section 9.17.)

104   Collaboration between institutions, particularly schools and colleges, should be encouraged to ensure that students can be offered a good range of GNVQ options, bearing in mind the need to ensure that the more capital-intensive subjects are covered. (Section 9.17.)

105 The manufacturing and engineering sectors of industry should give strong support to institutions in developing programmes in these areas. (Section 9.17.)

106 Additional units should be developed to extend the choice of units available to GNVQ students, so that they can direct their studies more closely to particular NVQs and build up the required knowledge and understanding underpinning them. (Section 9.19.)

107 There should be close and continuing monitoring of the experience of universities and of students who have gained places on the basis of the GNVQ. (Section 9.20.)

108 The regulatory and awarding bodies should develop units and qualifications which provide opportunities for applied learning at the proposed Entry level and progression to Foundation level. (Section 9.21.)

109 The NCVQ and the DfEE should work with the NVQ awarding bodies to secure rational and coherent provision in the interests of customers of the system. (Section 9.24.)

110 Because of concerns about the uneven quality of the tests, urgent consideration should be given to a unified test approved by NCVQ in advance of use. (Section 9.45.)

111 The role of external tests should be reconsidered to determine whether candidates should be required to answer questions covering the entire range of knowledge specified in a mandatory unit, whether the tests should be graded, and if so, the basis of grading. This review of the external tests should take account of what has been learned from the use of tests in the Part One GNVQ pilot and in particular the extent to which they test depth of understanding. (Section 9.46.)

112 If the use of tests to contribute to grading is validated through the Part One GNVQ pilot, this is one of the purposes for which they should be used. This would require testing depth of understanding and moving away from reliance exclusively on multiple choice questions. Higher levels of understanding are probably best assessed in other ways, requiring more extended answers than the selection of an answer offered in a multiple choice test. (Section 9.47.)

113 The Part One pilot has expanded the information available to teachers through explanatory notes on the GNVQ specifications. The NCVQ has now decided that this should be taken further, to provide a specification of the required knowledge and understanding. This practice should be extended (where it would be helpful) across the GNVQ generally, and SCAA, ACAC and CCEA should support this work. (Section 9.48.)

114 The NCVQ in conjunction with the vocational awarding bodies, should pursue the following proposals for increasing coherence in the field of school and college-based vocational training:

■ Map existing qualifications for which there is substantial demand on to GNVQs and NVQs to identify areas of overlap or close relationship.

■ Increase the pool of optional and additional units of GNVQs to allow for greater specialisation.

■ Consider greater flexibility in the structure of GNVQs, for example by reducing the number of mandatory units required in those awards without compromising comparability.

■ Take into account the implications of the proposal for six-unit awards based on the full GNVQ at Advanced level outlined elsewhere in this Report.

■ Consider the need for full GNVQs in new areas.

■ Look for ways of certificating existing qualifications as part of an NVQ or GNVQ. (Section 9.65.)

115 Links should be developed between the regulatory bodies and the National Open College Network to ensure that OCN accreditation leads to complementary local provision rather than a replication of national awards. (Section 9.66.)

The rigour of A levels, including policy towards modular examinations

116 There should be no reduction in the standards required in any subject. (Section 10.21.)

117 The awarding bodies should review the evidence prepared for this Report and reach agreed conclusions with the regulatory bodies. Where subjects seem decidedly below the 'average' level of difficulty, there should be a levelling-up of demand, after giving advance warning to institutions. Details of the procedure for bringing about this change should be agreed between the regulatory and awarding bodies and be subject to the approval of the Secretaries of State. (Section 10.21.)

118 The awarding bodies should ensure that standards are equivalent through their internal and collective procedures. (Section 10.26.)

119 The regulatory bodies should have the final responsibility to ensure that all is well. (Section 10.26.)

120 Each school and college should have a formal procedure, involving the head/principal of the institution, before a decision is taken to change an awarding body. (Section 10.26.)

121 The regulatory bodies, working in partnership with the awarding bodies, should reduce the number of syllabuses and options to levels where it is practical for them to be satisfied that equal standards prevail without requiring an unreasonable level of resources for the task, while preserving a reasonable choice for centres. (Section 10.37.)

122 With a reduction in the number of syllabuses and options, the resources thus released should be devoted to ensuring consistency of standards. (Section 10.37.)

123 The Secretaries of State should consider implementing Section 24 of the 1988 Education Reform Act which allows them to approve qualifications and a designated body to approve syllabuses. Implementation would give the designated regulatory body the power to control the number of syllabuses and content, if needed. (Section 10.37.)

124 The awarding bodies should maintain a comprehensive archive of examination papers, scripts, mark schemes, coursework, examination statistics and awards so that there is a better basis than at present to assess standards over time. The basis of this archive should be agreed between the regulatory and awarding bodies. (Section 10.44.)

125 Similar archives for checking standards over time should be set up for GNVQs, taking into account their distinctive characteristics, and what it would be feasible to retain and the effects on schools and colleges. The basis of this archive should be agreed between the awarding bodies and NCVQ. (Section 10.44.)

126 In addition to the annual checks of standards, the regulatory bodies (in association with the awarding bodies) should undertake an in-depth review of standards, so that over five years all subjects are covered, to ensure that standards are being maintained over time and across boards. (Section 10.44.)

127 The regulatory bodies should monitor closely the comparability and consistency of standards in modular and traditional linear A levels and publish an annual report on this. (Section 10.61.)

128 Consideration should be given to the approach outlined in Section 10.60 (combining features from linear and modular A levels into a unified approach) which, if the take-up of the traditional linear A level declines sharply, might become a standard form for A levels in the longer term. (Section 10.61.)

129 In the meantime, both traditional linear and modular A levels should be retained, but:

- The final examination in a modular scheme of assessment should count for not less than 30 per cent of the total marks and should include a number of questions, for which at least half the marks (15 per cent of the total marks for the A level) are reserved, that test understanding of the syllabus as a whole. (No changes are recommended for the traditional linear A level in this respect).

- There should be a limit on the number of re-sits of any one module, to be determined by the regulatory bodies after consultation with the awarding bodies.

■ The regulatory bodies should monitor closely whether it is possible to maintain a stream of fresh questions for modular examinations to avoid easy question-spotting, particularly in early modules.

■ The joint committee of the NCVQ and SCAA, with the involvement of Wales and Northern Ireland, should consider whether there should be a common timetable for modular examinations, based on two sittings a year, probably in January and June. They should consider this issue in consultation with the awarding bodies, considering at the same time the timing of GNVQ tests. (Section 10.61.)

130 The regulatory bodies should examine the extent to which it is practical and advantageous to take further the specification of A levels in terms of required learning outcomes. (Section 10.65.)

Mathematics and the sciences

131 Schools and colleges should encourage students proposing to take A level mathematics to take a GCSE paper in additional mathematics, whether equivalent in weight to a GCSE short course or a full GCSE. (Section 10.77.)

132 The regulatory bodies should encourage awarding bodies to seek approval under Section 5 of the Education Act 1988, so that the existing certificates in mathematics can form a new challenging GCSE course in additional mathematics, limited to grades A*–C. (Section 10.77.)

133 The regulatory bodies should review the range of curriculum material available to support courses to bridge the gap between GCSE and A level and, if necessary, stimulate the development of additional materials. (Section 10.77.)

134 The regulatory bodies, noting the concerns expressed in consultation about inadequate coverage of important areas of mathematics (see Section 10.71), drawing on the advice of the consultation group established by SCAA and the results obtained in due course from the study of standards over time, should enter into discussion with the awarding bodies about the requirements for A level mathematics including the size of the mandatory core. (Section 10.82.)

135 Schools and colleges should encourage students to make more use of further mathematics courses through which students can supplement the main A level course. If double mathematics is not practicable, a further mathematics course equal in weight to the AS would be of benefit. (Section 10.82.)

136 The regulatory bodies should enter into discussions with the awarding bodies to maintain a good range of options while reducing overlapping provision. (Section 10.82.)

137 The regulatory bodies should investigate the feasibility of devising A level mathematics courses targeted at specific levels of attainment, or containing content designed for specific purposes. (Section 10.82.)

138 The regulatory bodies should collect evidence to establish whether the current range of GCSE courses in the sciences satisfactorily provides both broad science education and sufficient preparation for further study at A level, and report their conclusions to the Secretaries of State. (Section 10.89.)

139 Schools should use 20% of curriculum time for double science, as urged by the Royal Society. (Section 10.89.)

140 The regulatory bodies should enter into discussions with the awarding bodies with a view to increasing the size of the A level subject core in the sciences and reducing the number of syllabuses currently available, while maintaining some scope for a range of syllabuses. (Section 10.95.)

141 Awarding bodies should note the comments that some of the more demanding content of syllabuses does not feature sufficiently in examinations. (Section 10.95.)

142 SCAA should assess the provision for chemistry in the light of the outcome of the OFSTED/ SCAA study of standards over time. (Section 10.95.)

143 Building upon the work of the Teacher Training Agency (TTA), the regulatory bodies should develop a programme of further research into factors affecting the attitudes of parents, pupils and teachers to mathematics and the sciences, and disseminate the findings through a programme of regional conferences, newsletters and other publications for schools. (Section 10.99.)

144 The regulatory bodies and the TTA should identify and disseminate measures arising from this research to encourage a greater take-up of mathematics and the sciences. (Section 10.99.)

145 Interactive learning packages of high quality designed for use in schools and colleges merit the kind of development that has been taking place in universities. (Section 10.99.)

146 SCAA's mathematics and science consultative group should explore further the issues considered in this section of the Report, with a view to some early decisions and action, and guide SCAA and ACAC in further research and policy development. ACAC and CCEA should consider parallel action in Wales and Northern Ireland respectively. (Section 10.99.)

147 The NCVQ should continue to consult with universities and employers to monitor the progress of the science GNVQ closely, so that its quality and fitness for purpose are assured, with a view to the GNVQ at Advanced level providing an additional source of scientists and science technicians. (Section 10.104.)

A reformulated AS

148 A new AS should be developed as a means of encouraging greater breadth of study in full-time 16–19 education and training and to reduce wastage for students who do not proceed to the full A level. Those intending to take the full A level could, if they wished, progress to it without taking the AS. (Section 11.22.)

149 The new AS should be graded on an A–E scale like the full A level, with the top grade defined as the standard attained by a student who, with one year's further study, would be expected to achieve grade A in the full A level; the other grades would relate to the A level standard in the same way... (Section 11.22.)

150 The content of the new AS should be the equivalent of half a full A level course (designed to occupy half the teaching time of a typical two-year advanced level course, or three modules out of six in a modular scheme). (Section 11.22.)

151 The new AS should count as half an A level in terms of performance tables, the proposed new UCAS tariff and the National Targets for Education and Training. (Section 11.22.)

152 The new AS should be re-named as 'Advanced Subsidiary' (AS)... (Section 11.22.)

153 The current AS and A level subject cores should be reviewed and, where necessary, revised to position the AS core as the 'foundation', with additional A level content expressed as 'extension' material... (Section 11.22.)

154 Where the AS provides directly for progression to either A levels or GNVQs, the first module or unit of the new AS should be based on common content drawn from the full award... (Section 11.22.)

155 The regulatory bodies should examine the case for new AS cores in a small number of subjects which are not normally offered pre-16 (for example, psychology, philosophy or economics) and in some which are currently not available but which might make a particular contribution to 'breadth' (for example, economic and industrial understanding, environmental education, European awareness, and citizenship). (Section 11.22.)

156 The current AS should be phased out as the new AS can be introduced, since to retain it would only add to confusion and complexity. (Section 11.22.)

157 The regulatory bodies should undertake a pilot study immediately to assess the implications for different subjects of a reformulated AS, including the timetabling and likely resource issues for schools and colleges of offering such courses... (Section 11.22.)

Recognising a wider range of achievement

158 Priority should be given to approving existing awards that develop key skills at Entry level; over time, the provision should become much wider than these to encompass the many valuable programmes which are offered at this level. (Section 12.15.)

159 The key criteria for approving or kitemarking awards at Entry level should be the following.

■ The units of award should be clearly specified in terms of learning outcomes which describe in a clear language what the learner is expected to know, understand and do as a result of achieving the unit.

■ The award should be designed to provide opportunities for progression to higher levels.

■ The awarding body should have adequate internal quality assurance mechanisms for its processes.

■ The awarding body should have a commitment to equal access. (Section 12.16.)

160 Any award below grade G in GCSE and the Foundation level of the GNVQ that meets the national standards prescribed by the regulatory bodies, should qualify for a certificate confirming that it is a National Award at Entry level. (Section 12.23.)

161 To be recognised as a National Award at Entry level, an award should be designed to offer progression to Foundation level. (Section 12.23.)

162 In accrediting such national awards, priority should be given in the short term to awards in communication, application of number and information technology... (Section 12.23.)

163 In order to facilitate this accreditation, consideration should be given to implementing the powers in Section 24 of the Education Reform Act. (Section 12.23.)

164 Students should have opportunities to take approved GNVQ units at Foundation and Intermediate levels from 14 onwards, as well as Entry level qualifications. (Section 12.33.)

165 SCAA and ACAC, should consider, together with the NCVQ, which NVQs, or NVQ units might be appropriate. These could then be approved for use in schools under Section 5 of the Education Reform Act.

166 Further support should be given at national level to existing initiatives designed to provide motivation and opportunity among under-achievers where traditional education has not succeeded. While school will provide the centre for 14–16 year old students' continued development, education related to the adult world, with opportunities for group and project work, offers potential for those who fail to see any point or relevance to school or a traditional academic curriculum. This is especially so if a part of the student's development post-14 can be in a different environment, such as a college of further education, the workplace, or simulations of it. The central objective should reflect concern to serve students well in ways that are meaningful to them whilst maintaining the entitlement to the statutory curriculum. (Section 12.39.)

167 Courses to accredit skills for independent adult life should be developed against, or revised to meet, nationally recognised criteria, drawn up by the regulatory bodies with approval from the Secretaries of State....These should be at the Entry level in the proposed National Framework, but consideration should be given to the need for further qualifications in those skills at higher levels, to provide progression routes. (Section 12.51.)

168 In addition the regulatory bodies should devise simple quality assurance measures for schemes to accredit small, worthwhile steps of progress by those with severe learning difficulties. (Section 12.51.)

169   Special Papers should be retained, with each awarding body agreeing to take responsibility for a number of subjects in order to secure cost-effective provision. (Section 12.85.)

170   Consideration should be given to developing approaches to the Special Papers based on A level subject cores, which will bring them within the range of the teaching resources of more institutions. (Section 12.85.)

171   Once the Special Paper has been reformulated, consideration should be given to recognising achievement through the proposed new UCAS tariff. (Section 12.85.)

172   In the interests of stability, a commitment should be made to provide reconstituted Special Papers for at least four years. (Section 12.85.)

173   As an alternative to the present approach, consideration should be given to externally extended assignments in which students research and explain a topic or an issue in depth. (Section 12.85.)

174   Schools and universities should take advantage of opportunities available through arrangements such as Associate Student Schemes, to enable students to take units of university courses while at school or college. This will give them credit towards their undergraduate studies, as well as providing an opportunity to extend their areas of interest. With such arrangements, in a few cases it may not be unrealistic to contemplate a first degree being completed in two years. (Section 12.85.)

175   Schools and colleges should be encouraged to extend the range of studies available to students through additional AS or A levels, or units of GNVQs or NVQs (where appropriate opportunities can be provided) to broaden the nature of their studies. The proposal in Section 5 of this Report for a new challenging option which combines depth with breadth of study and which would be available in all three pathways, is relevant in this context. (Section 12.85.)

176   For those pursuing an NVQ, apart from taking units from another closely-related vocation, the best approach may lie in providing for certification of the underpinning knowledge and understanding required for the next level of the NVQ, or in encouraging trainees to study either an AS in a relevant area (eg an AS in mathematics for an NVQ level 3 engineer), or modules from a university course. (Section 12.85.)

177   For GNVQ students, there are currently available opportunities to take additional units at the Advanced level, or AS or A levels. (Section 12.85.)

178   Consideration should be given to the content and role of a General Studies A level that will have standing with universities and attract a numerical score in the proposed new UCAS tariff. (Section 12.85.)

179   An element in such a development, or a free-standing development, might be a course equivalent in weight to a Special Paper, a module or unit in a General Studies A level, or even an AS qualification, aimed at developing a critical understanding of the various forms of knowledge. (Section 12.85.)

180   Students should be encouraged to pursue opportunities outside their main curriculum to develop their personal qualities through, for example, the Duke of Edinburgh's Award Scheme, Young Enterprise or work in the community (Section 12.85.)

The spiritual and moral dimension of 16–19 education

181   Regulatory and awarding bodies should recognise the potential relevance of spiritual and moral issues to individual subjects, particularly when designing and approving syllabuses. (Section 13.6.)

182   All providers of education and training should take spiritual and moral issues into account in the design and delivery of the curriculum and programmes for young people. (Section 13.6.)

Removing barriers to achievement

183   To monitor achievement, high quality, continuously up-dated information is needed both at the level of individual institutions and nationally for action to be taken. Present arrangements do not appear to be adequate and I recommend that they are reviewed. (Section 14.12.)

184   Excellent, independent careers education and guidance should be provided to all young people on their choice of pathways and their potential level of achievement, recognising the central role of local partnerships between schools, colleges and the careers service. Continued updating of knowledge should be provided to those giving advice, including issues relevant to maintaining equal opportunities. (Section 14.35.)

185   The regulatory, awarding and industry lead bodies should consider the issues relating to access to qualifications as part of their work on quality assurance, including:

- the specification of content (audit of content for clarity, cultural and linguistic bias);

- assessment arrangements (special arrangements, preparation and timing of assessments);

- guidance to centres (for example on equipment and learning support). (Section 14.35.)

186   Awarding bodies should include criteria on accessibility and training in related issues as part of revised Codes of Practice and centre approval criteria. (Section 14.35.)

187   Regulatory, awarding bodies, and lead bodies should continue to review the extent to which the content and arrangements for all forms of assessment need to be designed in ways that maintain standards but give equality of opportunity for all to demonstrate their achievement, independent of gender, racial origin, socio-economic group or disability, with research being commissioned as required to verify that there are no unnecessary obstacles to achievement. (Section 14.35.)

188   The regulatory bodies (and other appropriate agencies) should work together to develop a framework for monitoring and reporting nationally on candidate achievement by gender, racial origin, socio-economic group, disability or learning difficulty. (Section 14.35.)

189   The Government departments, regulatory and awarding bodies, Further Education Funding Councils, FEDA and other appropriate bodies should further investigate reasons for non-completion of awards (including the influence of external factors such as financial pressures, employment circumstances, personal problems, and the quality of the learning experience). They should improve the reliability of information on completion and destinations of all leavers. (Section 14.35.)

190   The regulatory bodies should explore (with employer bodies, Government departments and others) ways of encouraging an expansion of work experience opportunities. (Section 14.35.)

191   Schools and colleges should maximise the potential of information technology to improve their monitoring and tracking of students. (Section 14.35.)

Action

192   The recommendations in this Report to strengthen qualifications are interdependent with those of the Capey Committee and the Beaumont Review. Action on these recommendations should be co-ordinated by Government departments to minimise the burden on institutions, the awarding bodies and providers of education and training. (Section 15.1.)

193   In the light of the Government's response to this Report, the Department for Education and Employment, Welsh Office and Northern Ireland Office should consult with the regulatory and awarding bodies, other Government departments and the inspectorates, Further Education Funding Councils (England and Wales), Further Education Development Agency and the Teacher Training Agency on the implications of the Report and on a joint agenda for action. (Section 15.1.)

194 In recognition of the emphasis placed by all parties in consultation upon the need to raise national standards in the key skills of communication, the application of number and information technology, and the value attached by employers to personal and inter-personal skills, these should be included in the priorities in the joint agenda for action. (Section 15.1.)

195 With the continued growth of post-16 education and training, and the wider range of opportunities being offered in the applied and vocational pathways, consideration will need to be given at all levels to the curriculum that schools and colleges of different sizes can realistically provide and manage effectively within the resources available. (Section 15.1.)

196 Further consideration should be given to the case for more specific criteria for courses of initial teacher training which cover the 14–19 phase in schools. (Section 15.3.)

197 The implications of this Report for programmes of in-service education and training for teachers in schools should also be considered. (Section 15.3.)

198 Further consideration should be given to whether, in the light of the outcome of the deliberations of the Further Education Staff Development Forum, there is scope for further measures for the initial and continuing training of teachers and trainers not in schools. (Section 15.3.)

Abbreviations

A level   Advanced level

ACAC   Awdurdod Cwricwlwm Ac Asesu Cymru
Curriculum and Assessment Authority for Wales

ALIS   A Level Information Service

AS   Advanced Supplementary (to be renamed Advanced Subsidiary)

ASDAN   Award Scheme Development and Accreditation Network

ATL   Association of Teachers and Lecturers

BTEC   Business and Technology Education Council

CBI   Confederation of British Industry

CCEA   Council for the Curriculum, Examinations and Assessment (Northern Ireland)

CoE   Certificate of Education (Wales)

CUCP   Committee of Vice-Chancellors and Principals of the Universities of the United Kingdom

CSYS   Certificate of Sixth Year Studies

DENI   Department of Education Northern Ireland

DfEE   Department for Education and Employment

DoA   Diploma of Achievement

EAG   Evaluation Advisory Group

FE   Further Education

FEDA   Further Education Development Agency

FEFC   Further Education Funding Council

FEU   Further Education Unit

GCE   General Certificate of Education

GCSE   General Certificate of Secondary Education

GNVQ   General National Vocational Qualification

HE   Higher Education

IT   Information Technology

ITO	Industry Training Organisation
LB	Lead Body
LEA	Local Education Authority
LEC	Local Enterprise Company
NCVQ	National Council for Vocational Qualifications
NDPB	Non-Departmental Public Body
NFER	National Foundation for Educational Research
NLS	National Language Standards
NRA	National Record of Achievement
NVQ	National Vocational Qualification
O level	Ordinary level
OCN	Open College Network
OFSTED	Office for Standards in Education
S Paper	Special Paper
SAC	Subject Advisory Committee
SCAA	School Curriculum and Assessment Authority
SCOTVEC	Scottish Vocational Education Council
SCPR	Social and Community Planning Research
SEB	Scottish Examinations Board
SEN	Special Educational Needs
SVQ	Scottish Vocational Qualification
TEC	Training and Enterprise Council
TTA	Teacher Training Agency
UCAS	Universities and Colleges Admissions Service
UCCA	Universities Central Council on Admissions
WJEC	Welsh Joint Education Committee
WOED	Welsh Office Education Department